SOMEWHERE ON THE BORDER

SOMEWHERE ON THE BORDER

ANTHONY AKERMAN

AFTERWORD BY GARY BAINES

WITS UNIVERSITY PRESS

Published in South Africa by:

Wits University Press
1 Jan Smuts Avenue
Johannesburg
2001

www.witspress.co.za

Somewhere on the Border was first published by Nick Hern Books in 1993 in an anthology titled *South Africa Plays: New South African Drama* edited by Stephen Gray.

ISBN 978-1-86814-560-7

Application to perform this work in public and to obtain a copy of the play should be made to: Dramatic, Artistic and Literary Rights Organisation (DALRO), P O Box 31627, Braamfontein, 2017.
No performance may be given unless a licence has been obtained.

Edited by Pat Tucker
Cover design and page layout by Hothouse South Africa
Cover photograph by Suzy Bernstein
Printed and bound by Creda Communications

For my wife
André Hattingh

Contents

Preface[1]

Anthony Akerman

When I was 16 and received my call-up to serve in the South African Defence Force I didn't realise I was being asked to defend an ideology rather than a sovereign state. Because of censorship and the banning of opposition political movements during the 1960s I grew up largely unaware of the major ideological confrontation in the country. Going to the army was a daunting prospect, but it didn't have any political implications for me. I was called up in the last year of the ballot system. Some of my friends didn't have to go. I was one of the unlucky ones. If I hadn't been unlucky, I wouldn't have written *Somewhere on the Border*.

The first thing you learnt in the army was not to draw attention to yourself and not to volunteer for anything. I tried to keep my nose clean, but had little genuine respect for military rules and regulations. As a result, I was caught with cigarettes and matches while guarding the ammunition dump at Jan Kemp Dorp, put on orders and marched into a major's office. I was slightly blindsided when the major asked me if I didn't love my country. He then explained how my cigarette could have blown up Jan Kemp Dorp, which, in turn, would have blown up Kimberley, which would have then, I think, ignited an ammunition dump near Bloemfontein and the end result would have been a national conflagration. With people like me in the army, who needed the *swart gevaar* [black peril]? I was given ten extra drills as a punishment.

The next time I was placed on orders was when I was a first-year student at the University of Natal in Pietermaritzburg. By then I was *gatvol* [fed-up] with the army and hadn't realised that my citizen force unit, the Natal Field Artillery, would be calling me up for monthly parades at the Drill Hall. A part-time field cornet, determined to reverse the decadent trend of long hair sweeping across the world, put me on orders because my hair was longer than the bristles on a standard issue toothbrush and, once again, I was given extra duties. After that, I made a vow that I'd never wear an army uniform again.

I persuaded my father to send me to Rhodes University because it had a good English Department. The real reason was that Grahamstown was far removed from the Natal Field Artillery and so I couldn't be made to do monthly parades. I spent my four years at Rhodes concocting plausible, if not scrupulously honest, excuses to evade three-week camps. By 1973 I'd run out of excuses. I was ordered to report for a camp in June. At the age of 23 I had more outspoken political views and I wasn't going to serve in an army that was there to enforce an ideology I now regarded as indefensible and inhuman. Although our actions are always prompted by multiple motives I left South Africa in April 1973, in large part because of the army. I didn't return for 17 years.

Fast forward nine years and you find me living in a 17th-century house in the red-light district in Amsterdam, integrated into Dutch society, speaking Dutch most of the time and working as a director in Dutch theatre. There was also a fairly large South African exile community and, yes, some of my best friends were South Africans.

After Britain and the Netherlands decided to give political asylum to white South African males with call-up papers for Angola a steady stream of conscripts took this option. Asylum seekers were assisted by the Committee on South African War Resistance and in 1981 Michael Smith, one of their organisers, asked if I'd write a play for them. I didn't have the time, I was wary of writing propaganda if that's what they were asking for, even if it was counter-propaganda, but the real reason was, I suppose, that I'd never written a play and didn't know whether I could. So I passed.

But Michael's request had planted a seed and I started thinking about an army play. In the late 1970s I'd seen a photograph taken after the South African raid on Cassinga, Angola. Professor Gary Baines of the Rhodes University History Department has written lucidly about how the propaganda battle for Cassinga is still being waged[2] but in the 1970s I accepted claims by international journalists that Cassinga was a Namibian refugee camp and that the number of casualties, most of them civilians, could have been as high as 1 000.

I also watched, with deep distrust, a video of South African television coverage of Operation Reindeer, the military codename for the attack on Cassinga, in turn codenamed Moscow. After all, the South African Broadcasting Corporation was his master's voice. The photograph I saw was of a mass grave and, among the bodies, were women and children. I ended my programme note to the first production of *Somewhere on the Border* with these words: 'So when I look at that photograph – with all my feelings of revulsion, compassion and shame – I am left with a single thought: 'there, but for the grace of God, was I.'

My play started with that image and the thought that, regardless of my values and beliefs, I could have been standing on the edge of that mass grave, wearing army browns and holding an R1 rifle. I had taken a different road. If I hadn't, that could have happened. Perhaps I felt vindicated for having gone into voluntary exile. It was certainly more comfortable, both physically and morally, but to write the play I had to travel a different journey in my imagination. So the backbone of the story is how Campbell, a young man who rejects racism and the military, surrenders territory inch by inch in order to survive and ultimately betrays everything he believes in, including himself.

I started working on characters and plot in March 1982. I'd obviously put quite a lot of thought into it because what I recorded in my notebook almost 30 years ago is not very different from what ultimately went into the play. To start with, I drew on my own experiences in the army for characters, situation and language.

We'd had a bombardier in Potchefstroom, a malevolent, pink-eyed bullterrier of a man, who took particular pleasure in persecuting my friend Andrew Campbell and pronouncing his name 'Kammel'.

Kotze started out as a composite of him and a staff sergeant who shouted at David Levitt, standing next to me in the platoon, 'Levitt, in Hitler's day we would have made soap out of you!' Enter Levitt and his anti-Semitic persecutors. I was also particularly interested in exploring a young Afrikaans character, someone with good values and a good heart, who has a Damascene experience. Of course his name had to be Paul.

I took the name Trevor Mowbray from a particularly feared local thug in my buzz-bike-riding youth and I have known many Badenhorsts, with their interminable jokes and stories of sexual exploits. The character called Black Actor is more of a Brechtian than a naturalistic character – a projection of white prejudice and fear, but it's also a part for an actor who progresses from servility through mockery and defiance to an avenging angel, freedom fighter and yet another casualty of war.

I also spoke to many people about their army experiences and many of their memories were folded into the texture of the play. In some cases it was a wonderfully graphic expression used by a sergeant or corporal such as, 'I'll stick your cock up your arse and carry you down to the station like a suitcase!'

Two people shared their experiences of the infamous Ward 22 at One Mil Hospital in Pretoria. One of them, who was a Durban dagga smoker, encountered people who had been given shock therapy for refusing to go to Angola[3] and saw someone attempting to cut through his own Achilles tendon with the saw blade of a Swiss army knife so he'd be discharged from the army. The other was given shock therapy by Colonel Aubrey Levin to cure him of his homosexuality.[4] A very significant contribution was made by one of the people I interviewed – Chris, a surfer from East London. He had served on the border and when, a year later, he was called up for another tour of duty he left the country the very next day. I have no idea where he is now, but we spent an afternoon together and I recorded his story.

The events towards the end of *Somewhere on the Border* are, in a sense, authentic, because they actually happened to him. He had been up on the border for five months and nothing had happened. The day before he was due to return home a rocket attack was launched on his base. He'd just got up to stand-to at first light. He said he heard bangs, 'and then these things came screaming in. There was a direct hit on the bungalow' where he'd been sleeping half an hour before. 'Guys were blown to nothing.' He described his best friend as looking 'like a charred ember.' He talked about 'severed feet in boots, heads in helmets. You get to know fear, man.'

In a matter of hours they were across the border. He said, 'When you see your friends getting killed, it gets to you. You only think of killing.' They got stoned before going into action. 'If your number comes up, it comes up. It's something you just can't worry about.' He spoke of things he witnessed. 'The killing frenzy. The absolute power. Shooting people down who had their hands up, surrendering.' He, too, had killed people. He was only 18 at the time. How different this was from the sanitised and saccharine version being served up to the South African public on *Springbok Radio Rendezvous* and *Forces Favourites*. But it was from those programmes that I found my title *Somewhere on the Border*.

There was a moment when I wondered why, having left the country nine years previously, I was becoming so obsessed by this subject and so committed to writing this play. After all, I had already submitted an application for Dutch citizenship. Then I received a brown envelope in the post, bearing the stamp of Defence Headquarters in Pretoria. It was a form for the Annual Registration of Reservists. Apparently I was still a reservist in the South African Defence Force. That settled the matter. If I'd ever been in doubt, it *was* still my problem.

I knew the play I wanted to write would not find favour with the Directorate of Publications in South Africa. Censorship was something every South African writer had to come to terms with. Having a book banned after publication, or a play banned after opening night, could be financially ruinous. Publishers and theatres would seek legal guidance on what could and could not be said and, as some writers pointed out, self-censorship was insidious and potentially a greater threat to freedom of expression than the Directorate of Publications.

The title I had chosen was, significantly, itself an expression of censored language. You sent a message to someone 'somewhere on the border' because the exact location was shrouded in official secrecy. However, as I planned to stage the play in the Netherlands with a South African cast, I felt I could tell it like it was. One of the first things I wanted to do was use the language spoken in the army. No films or plays I'd seen had ever done that and I felt it was a manifestation of the way the men in the masculine world of the military felt about women. But there's no getting away from it: I've written a play that's not suitable for polite company.

Although I felt I would never have been able to write the play the way I wrote it had I been living in South Africa, people who read early drafts encouraged me to believe a production there was within the realm of possibility. The Market Theatre, Johannesburg, for example, was producing work that was critical of the system and getting away with it. Tony Peake[5], a South African friend who had just established a small literary agency in London, asked if he could represent the play. At the time the Market Theatre's production of *Woza Albert!* was playing in the West End and I asked him to get the play to Market Theatre founder and the play's director, Barney Simon. Unfortunately, Barney declined to produce the play and it has taken 30 years to get it on a stage at the Market Theatre.

Although I was now committed to finding funding for a production in the Netherlands, I was still excited at the prospect of a South African production. I also got the play to a small publishing house called Taurus Press, which had been established in 1973 by several writers and academics[6] from the Afrikaans Department at the University of the Witwatersrand and was committed to publishing work turned down by commercial publishing houses because of the financial risk involved if the work was banned.

In 1983 Brendan Boyle, who was working for United Press International in Amsterdam at the time, handed me a telex that read, 'the play *Somewhere on the Border* by Anthony Akerman was banned in September.' [For illustrations of these documents and correspondence between the author and the Directorate of Publications, see pages xxx–xxxv]. It would be disingenuous to say I was surprised, but nonetheless I was shocked. A copy of the play I'd posted to Athol Fugard never arrived. Clearly, someone else was reading his post and that person must have submitted my play to the Directorate of Publications.

I suppose having a play banned by the apartheid government meant I must have been doing something right. My Dutch activist friends even congratulated me. I knew I had written a play that would be banned if examined by the censors, but now that had happened I realised a door had been slammed shut. I'd allowed myself to hope the play could be seen at home by a South African audience. Now I'd been deprived of that audience and the experience was profoundly alienating. Censorship is always political and anyone who has experienced it at first hand it will forever be implacably opposed to any legislation aimed at stifling freedom of expression.

The play opened with a South African cast in The Hague on 11 November 1983, which was appropriately, if fortuitously, Armistice Day. Even my stage manager, Johnny, was a South African who had been given asylum as a war resister. He was from a conservative Afrikaans background and had had a troubled childhood, much of which had been spent in Tokai Reformatory. He went AWOL [absent without official leave] in the army, was caught by the military police, slashed his wrists, was stitched up and was then sent to detention barracks for a month.

Johnny did the lighting and I operated the sound and we sat next to each other in the box at each performance. He connected with the character of Paul Marais and I watched him holding back his tears every night in the final scene. In 1999 I was told he'd been a spy. I wrote to him and he confirmed it and explained that when he came out of DB [detention barracks], he went AWOL again, living below the radar as did many people evading conscription. His girlfriend was a friend of Lisa Williamson, spy boss Craig Williamson's sister. She offered to wipe the slate clean if he worked for the security police, so he was sent to the Netherlands to apply for political asylum as a war resister and infiltrate their movement.

He wrote, 'So yes, I was employed by the S.A. police at the time of *Somewhere on the Border*. I can't say anything with certainty, but I doubt if anything I reported at that time could have had much influence. I didn't report anything that wouldn't have been in the Dutch media long before, and I didn't really have time for anything but the play at the time. If my role played any part in any of the difficulties you had with the S.A. embassy, I'm deeply sorry.' Johnny still lives in Amsterdam and we're Facebook friends.

The production was well received in The Netherlands. If Dutch audiences were horrified by the violence and racism they were also confused by the laughter it elicited from South Africans, especially black South Africans, in the audience.

The banning of the script put paid to any hopes of publication. Before I had seen the *Government Gazette*, I had written to Ampie Coetzee at Taurus Press to tell him what had happened. In February 1984 he replied:

I've contacted the Centre for Applied Legal Studies [at Wits University] and they can't find any record of the banning in

Jacobsen's List (of 'objectionable lit'!) [*sic*]⁷. So what we think is that you should write to the Directorate of Publications and find out if it's factually true. If it is, we would like to have the info for *Stet* our little lit. mag. But we don't want to write to them because we don't communicate with them – and they know it and they are very sensitive about it.

That helped me overcome the resistance I felt about communicating with what I felt was a contaminated organ of the state. In May 1984 I wrote, saying I'd seen the notice in the *Government Gazette* stating the play had been banned, inquiring how they had come to be in possession of the script and asking for a detailed list of all the offending passages. I received a prompt reply:

> The script was examined as a publication and not as a public entertainment and after examining the publication the statutory Committee of Publications gave the following reasons for their decision: 'The language used in the book is not only vulgar but will be offensive to the reasonable and balanced reader and is therefore undesirable within the meaning of section 47 (2) (a) of the Act. See the following, pages in brackets: fuck off (3), cunt-eyed (3), arse (5), dumb cunt (7), shit (7), moer (8), shit (8), I'll pull a cow's cunt over your heand (*sic*) and let a bull fuck some sense into it (9)...'

The rehearsal script they had in their possession was about 80 pages long, but they obviously felt they had made their point and soon started flagging. As section 47(2)(a) was specifically designed to stem the tide of work that was 'harmful to public morals' I had to wonder how Mr S F du Toit, the Director of Publications, had been able to type this letter without himself being dragged down into a cesspool of moral depravity. The statutory committee further opined that: 'In the closing parts of the book the South African Armed

Forces are placed in an extremely bad light and in this way it is undesirable within the meaning of section 47 (2) (e) of the Act.'

In terms of subsection (e) the work was 'deemed to be undesirable if it or any part of it is prejudicial to the safety of the state, the general welfare or the peace and good order'. Mr du Toit concluded, 'The script may not be distributed in the Republic of South Africa but a play could be staged if the parts which were found to be offensive are deleted.'

He didn't tell me how the board had come to be in possession of the script, so I wrote to him once again. He patiently explained that any person who desired a decision from the committee as to whether a work was undesirable could submit that work to the committee. He added, 'The Directorate does not however disclose the name of the submitter'.

That pretty much dashed my hopes of a South African production. But I did circulate the script as much as I could. I contacted several South African playwrights who I knew had also written plays set in the army and we swapped manuscripts. Looking back through correspondence I see there was sporadic interest in trying to put the play on in South Africa, but people were invariably deterred when they heard it was banned.

It was translated into German and Spanish and had a staged reading in New York, but not much else was happening. Nicholas 'Fink' Haysom, human rights lawyer and friend, was in Amsterdam and I solicited some free legal advice over a couple of beers. If the Directorate of Publications stipulated that the word 'fart' was undesirable on page 25 and they made no reference to its occurrence on page 30, could the word be spoken on page 30 without being offensive to reasonable and balanced people? And would you need to cut the final scene in order not to prejudice the safety of the state? Fink didn't venture a legal opinion, but that became academic when several actors working for the Performing Arts Council of the Orange Free State (PACOFS) in Bloemfontein decided to put on the play under their own banner.

Deon Opperman and I had exchanged army plays a couple of years previously and he asked for the performance rights. I alerted him to the fact that the play had been banned, but that didn't worry him. Gerrit Schoonhoven directed the production with, among others, Deon Opperman and A J van der Merwe[8]. I was told they rehearsed after hours and behind closed doors because they didn't want to alert the powers that be at PACOFS.

Although I didn't know it at the time, the play was considerably shortened to fit into a fringe slot. It opened at the Grahamstown Festival in 1986, during a State of Emergency when Casspirs (landmine-protected personnel carriers) prowled the streets. The production was highly acclaimed and sold out. I was told how boys who'd been on the border took their parents to see the play and after that were able, for the first time, to talk about what they'd been through. Jon White-Spunner, then manager of the Little Theatre in Cape Town, immediately booked a run and Bobby Heaney, then artistic director of the Performing Arts Council of the Transvaal (PACT), booked a season at the Alexander Theatre in Johannesburg.

A few years previously I'd renounced my South African citizenship in order to become a Dutch citizen. I hadn't been in South Africa for 13 years and now I wouldn't be allowed in without a visa. It was strange sitting in Amsterdam and thinking, 'at this very moment seven actors are performing my play, my *banned* play, and a South African audience is watching it – in South Africa.'

Not a word was heard from the Directorate of Publications, but less than an hour before one of the first performances in Cape Town military police, invoking a law prohibiting civilians from wearing SA Defence Force uniforms, raided the theatre and confiscated the army browns the actors were wearing as costumes. The actors wore overalls instead and ticket sales benefited from the press coverage the incident generated.

Hannes Muller, one of the actors in that production, recently told me that there were also no fewer than four bomb scares at different theatres during the run, although this obviously wasn't publicised for fear of encouraging copycats. One night in February 1987, after a performance in Johannesburg, two of the actors were driving along Showground Road (near Wits University)[9] when they were forced off the road by two cars. André-Jacques van der Merwe told the Johannesburg daily, *The Star*, 'I was driving in front of Mr Lombard, as he asked me to direct him to Ontdekkers Road. A BMW with about four occupants stopped in front of me. A man opened my car door and said, 'What is your story?' Then all of them began to hit me over and over again with their fists and rubber batons.'

André Lombard got out of his car to go to Van der Merwe's assistance when a Mazda with five or six occupants pulled up behind him. André Lombard told the newspaper that one of the men said, '*Jy wil mos speel, speel nou!* [You want to act, act now!][10] and then began to beat him. Lombard, who played Marais in the play, had to undergo surgery for a broken nose and Gerrit Schoonhoven took over his part for the rest of the Johannesburg run.

The actors laid a charge at the Brixton Police Station but couldn't remember the registration numbers of the cars. No arrest was ever made. From then on PACT employed a private security company to protect the cast. They were transported to and from the theatre by armed guards, who remained at the stage door during performances.

If there was ever any doubt in the actors' minds as to why they were attacked, the Hiemstra Commission gave them the answer in 1990. The commission was set up after a report in *The Star*, on what became known as the City Hall Spy Scandal. Evidence was given of cooperation between the Defence Force's Civil Co-Operation Bureau and the City Council's security department.

According to one witness, Johannes Gouws, former head of the Johannessburg City Council's Information Department, most of the department's employees were linked to the military in one way or another. He testified that a special unit was put together in 1986 and 1987 to carry out certain duties, among which was to intimidate opponents of the government. They also 'broke arms and legs.'

He went on to say, 'Among other things, a decision was taken to assault an actor in order to stop performances of a play in which the army was presented in a bad light.' Although this is my translation from a report in the Afrikaans newspaper, *Beeld*, it strikes me as interesting that the Directorate of Publications Board also referred to the armed forces being presented in 'a bad light.' Gouws couldn't remember the name of the actor or of the play, but said, 'it could have been the play *Somewhere on the Border*.' He added that many assignments were given by a Major Laubscher. So, the actors were employed by a state-subsidised theatre that in turn employed private security guards to protect them against other state employees. That's how taxpayers' money was being spent.

From Amsterdam, South Africa seemed a dark and dangerous place. And yet, after what had happened, perhaps perversely, I felt drawn towards the heart of darkness. When I left the country on 18 April 1973 I made a silent vow never to set foot in apartheid South Africa again. My refusal to come home for holidays had mystified my parents. Now, however, I decided I would no longer be held hostage by my impetuous and dogmatic 23-year-old self. So I applied for a visa.

In the past, the South African Embassy and I had enjoyed an uneasy relationship. When I needed to renew my passport in the late 1970s I was told by a member of the embassy staff who rejoiced in the name of Mr Bitzer that the process would take three months. When I asked why he said, 'You probably know the answer to that question better than we do.'

The answer was, no doubt, that I had met Connie Braam, head of the Dutch Anti-Apartheid Movement (AABN)[11] through African National Congress (ANC) friends in London and she had brought me to Amsterdam to write a chapter on censorship for a parliamentary report that eventually resulted in the Netherlands suspending its cultural agreement with South Africa.

But I'm sure Mr Bitzer knew that too. From then until I became a Dutch citizen Mr Bitzer and I went through an annual charade of waiting three months for my passport to be renewed. I tried to behave as if it was the most natural thing in the world, but had no difficulty renouncing my South African citizenship when the time came, in 1983. He is referred to as Baas Bitzer by the Black Actor in *Somewhere on the Border* and if he wants to know why, he probably knows the answer to that question better than I do.

I submitted my visa application and a few days later I received the inevitable phone call asking me to come for an interview. I drove down to The Hague on Monday 13 April 1987 and presented myself at the South African Embassy. Afterwards, for therapeutic reasons, I recorded the encounter in minute detail in my notebook, but the short version is that I had a lengthy interview with Miss Marina Minnie, a career diplomat and the second secretary, and a Mr de Meyer, who explained that he was there, in his words, for 'the legal side of things'.

We got off to a bad start when they said they were hurt by a remark I'd made to *Elsevier's Magazine*. I couldn't remember what I'd said and I started sweating when a very thick file was put on the table and a particular article was taken out to jog my memory. The gist of what I'd said was that I'd never return to South Africa until decency prevailed there, but the words I'd used in Dutch – '*fatsoenlijk land*' [decent country] – had cut them to the quick.

So, why did I want to go back now? Had I changed my mind or did I think South Africa had changed? I was hoist on my own petard and had to do some very fancy footwork around these issues in an attempt not to look like a total arse. They seemed to have a copy of every article I'd written and every interview I'd ever given and they had me on the back foot. They knew all about *Somewhere on the*

Border. The information they had was more exhaustive than they could have got from debriefing Johnny, my stage manager.

Years later, Andrew Campbell told me how, while on a military camp, he had been called into the commandant's office and had been left alone with two special branch men who had shown him a photograph of the two of us drinking a beer with Ronnie Kasrils, an ANC and Communist Party member, in London and one of us walking out of the offices of the AABN building in Amsterdam.

They offered him an air ticket to visit me and all he'd have to do in exchange was tell them anything he thought they'd want to know. Andrew declined their offer, but remembers the encounter as a chilling experience. The point is, it was impossible for me to bluff Miss Minnie or Mr de Meyer. They tried to engage me in a political debate. Mandela would be a free man if he would only renounce violence. They wanted me to agree with them. It crossed my mind to say that a political prisoner couldn't negotiate, but it wouldn't have helped my cause, as they would make the recommendation on my suitability for a South African visa. I wasn't sure about Mr de Meyer, but I liked Miss Minnie. She said brightly, assuming I'd get a visa, that if I went back to South Africa I'd probably want to live there again.

Then the wait began. My father's attorneys were in regular contact with the Ministry of Home Affairs in Pretoria, who seemed to be having considerable difficulty arriving at a decision on such a thorny issue. Of course, they were having their bit of fun. Eventually I had to delay my flight. The day before my original departure date De Meyer phoned me. My application had been refused. The decision 'came from the top', he said. My father, a kind and conservative man, allowed himself to think the authorities had behaved badly, but my mother's response typified her generation of white South African attitudes. 'Well, boykie,' she said, 'you must've done something wrong.'

I did my best to be stoical but one of my friends, the English playwright Howard Brenton, said, 'Anthony, that's bloody outrageous!'

He found it inconceivable that any British government could ever behave in such a way to one of its former citizens. Having grown up under an authoritarian government that deliberately blurred the distinction between the ruling party and the state I took no rights for granted. I had been brought up thinking things like passports were a privilege, a reward for conformist behaviour, and in spite of myself I'd accepted that. I'd allowed myself to be bullied. Howard was right, it was bloody outrageous. So I made sure reports on the matter appeared in both the South African and the Dutch press.

This decision changed my status. I was no longer in self-imposed exile, I was an exile; someone who was officially *persona non grata* with the South African state. So you might well imagine my surprise when, after the German-language premiere of *Somewhere on the Border* in Stuttgart, I received a request from Professor Dr D Morkel, the cultural attaché at the South African Embassy in Bonn, requesting a copy of the play 'in English or German and any other details you might think interesting.' What was he thinking?

I'm afraid I probably replied rather ungraciously and I sent his letter with a covering note to the Johannessburg newspaper the *Weekly Mail*, where it was reprinted in the humorous column *Krisjan Lemmer's Diary* with a tongue-in-cheek commentary which ended, 'Akerman is thoroughly confused, and who wouldn't be. He has two questions for the Minister of Home Affairs Stoffel Botha: a) Is it policy for SA's Embassies to collect banned literature? and b) Can he come home now?' I was also having my bit of fun.

While all this was happening my Dutch agent had got me onto the books of the legendary literary agent Margaret Ramsay. After reading *Somewhere on the Border* she agreed to take me on as a client. This was very exciting because Peggy, as she was known, was the most powerful agent in London. She was someone who could phone Laurence Olivier and say, 'Larry, I'm sending you a play. I want you to read it now and give me your answer by tomorrow morning.' And

Lord Olivier would do her bidding. In the second half of the 20th century she represented royalty among playwrights: J B Priestley, Tennessee Williams, Robert Bolt, David Mercer, Joe Orton, Edward Bond, Christopher Hampton, Howard Brenton, Alan Ayckbourn, Caryl Churchill, David Hare and Ben Elton, among many others.

This was exactly what my career needed. I spent a memorable two hours with her one afternoon in her little office off St Martin's Lane. Although she never disclosed her age, she was born in Australia in 1908. However, she'd had a South African childhood in Oudtshoorn and went to Rhodes, where, she told me, she eloped with a professor at the end of first year, went to London and became a chorus girl. It's a good story. She vamped it up, flirted and charmed me utterly, and she was all of 80.

Not long after that someone who'd seen Gerrit Schoonhoven's production phoned me in Amsterdam and asked for the rights because she wanted to film the production for Channel 4 television. I was excited and referred her to Peggy. She phoned me back a few minutes later in the state of shock. Peggy had blasted her in language that would have made Mr S F du Toit of the Directorate of Publications reach for his revolver. It turned out Peggy hated television and thought a filmed production of my play would put paid to its theatrical future. She was still going to get it a top-notch British production. But that was not to be and, sadly, not long after that Peggy's powers were considerably diminished by the Alzheimer's disease that eventually carried her off.

On 2 February 1990 Mr de Meyer and Miss Minnie would have had reason to sit up when President F W de Klerk made his watershed speech unbanning political organisations that had hitherto been regarded as verging on the satanic. Nelson Mandela was to be set free unconditionally. The day after he walked out of Victor Verster Prison in Cape Town, I made a point of applying for a visa. It was granted without delay or impertinent questions and Miss Minnie was right, it wasn't long before I decided I wanted to live in South Africa again.

In that year I directed *Somewhere on the Border* for the Natal Performing Arts Council's Loft Theatre company in Durban. We got the beds we needed from the army and the rifles from the police, but we couldn't get a *Playboy* magazine. I had one sent in from Amsterdam and it was confiscated by the post office. The early 1990s were a strange and edgy interregnum, but it was good to be home and it was good to do my play in the town where I was born.

But that's all in the past and, as L P Hartley famously wrote, 'The past is a foreign country: they do things differently there.'[12] In 1993 conscription was abolished and in 1994 *Somewhere on the Border* was published in London in an anthology called *South Africa Plays: New South African Drama*.[13] What was once harmful to public morals is now occasionally a school and university set work.

For the past two decades the prevailing political orthodoxy seems to have encouraged a kind of collective amnesia about the Border War. There were no war trials and the Truth and Reconciliation Commission grappled with the issue in a way that could best be described as unsatisfactory. Former military top brass wouldn't appear, although Laurie Nathan of the End Conscription Campaign did. He elaborated on the complexity of the issue, of how the apartheid system made conscripts both victims and perpetrators. As Theresa Edlmann, a doctoral student currently researching the psychological legacies of the SADF conscripts' experiences, pointed out in a recent paper, 'the TRC was designed in such a way as to designate people as victims *or* perpetrators. There was no legislative space for people who fitted into both categories.'[14] I've recently heard another aphorism about the past. It's new, anonymous and it seems to be going viral. 'The past is always with us, just waiting to mess with the present.'

An estimated 600 000 white males were conscripted into the South African Armed Forces between 1968 and 1993 and most of us are still alive. Many of those who went to war still bear the scars, physical, emotional and psychological. You can't wish them away. There is a noticeable resurgence of interest in the Border War, evidenced in the plethora of recent publications, as well as Afrikaans television programme Kyk-Net's 26-part documentary series called *Grensoorlog* [Border War]. When it was first screened in 2008 the series apparently attracted a record number of viewers to the channel and it was rebroadcast in 2011.

The Border War has become a field of considered academic investigation and has also led to an acrimonious and polarising clash between self-interested lobby groups on the one hand and the inconsistent ideological postures adopted by the trustees of Freedom Park[15] on the other.

I wrote *Somewhere on the Border* because I wanted to expose some unpalatable truths about the military and a war that state propaganda presented to South Africans as both unavoidable and just. The fact that black soldiers were enlisted to fight in the SADF and that the enemy was supported by Cuban troops and Soviet weapons doesn't alter the fact that the war was being fought to preserve minority white rule in South Africa.

Although I wrote the play as a protest I never felt what I had written had any stylistic similarity to what, in the 1980s, was loosely called protest theatre. It's a character-driven drama in the realist tradition. But the explosive subject matter, the banning of the script, the confiscation by the military police of the actors' uniforms, bomb scares and actors being attacked by a hit squad would all have contributed to its being perceived as a so-called protest play. At the time it was one of the voices raised against the brutalisation of the South African military and I'm still proud of that.

But how do audiences relate to it today? In 2009 it was staged at Pretoria Boys High School with a cast of schoolboys who would all have been born after the Border War ended. It was directed by Amanda van Zyl, head of art and culture at the school, and the rumblings of dissent that emanated from some staff members and the proverbial 'concerned parents' demonstrated that the play had not lost its controversial edge. As a result, Amanda had a two-year struggle to put the play on, something she said she wouldn't have been able to do without the commitment of her schoolboy actors.

Understandably, the language was toned down and had Mr S F du Toit attended the performance he would not have been out of his comfort zone. I spoke to some of the fathers in the audience watching their sons re-enact something they had lived through. The fathers were the boys who went to the border and we had come full circle. The play could now be the catalyst for a new generation of fathers and sons to talk about the war.

After seeing this production my wife insisted it was time the play had a professional revival. I approached Ismail Mahomed, director of the National Arts Festival, and submitted a proposal. The festival funded André Odendaal's production, which opened in Grahamstown 25 years after the first South African production. The play still resonates with the younger generation and the actors, none of whom was born when I wrote the play, are all so committed that they have become co-producers of the production that opens at the Market Theatre in 2012.

What I hadn't foreseen was the way in which the play would resonate with veterans of the Border War, many of whom were sent into combat against their will and are now struggling to find psychological and spiritual healing. Peter Frost, editor of the festival publication *Cue* and a student during the 1980s, focused on this fact and the words with which he ended his review are unmistakably a *cri de coeur* from his generation.

> This trauma, the fallout from those scarring years, has not received the attention it deserves in a democratic South Africa, for arguably understandable reasons. But the legacy of this play, finally, after all these years, performed right now, here, is massively positive. For

an army of 40+ men (and their families) battling the consequences of latent rage, this is an acknowledgement that their history is not incidental, despite the context of their tragedy. Good news. Nothing stunts healing like disregard. Ask this country's other Lost Generation.

Johannesburg, November 2011.

NOTES

1 A slightly different version of this preface was presented as a public lecture on 8 July at Think!Fest during the National Arts Festival 2011.

2 Gary Baines, 'The Battle for Cassinga: Conflicting Narratives and Contested Meanings', Basler Afrika Bibliographien Seminar, Basel, Switzerland, 11 December 2007. Available at: www.baslerafrika.ch/upload/files/WP_2007_2__Baines.pdf. Also available at: eprints.ru.ac.za/946/01/baines_Cassinga.pdf

3 Campbell uses some of his words in the play when he describes his own experience in One Mil Hospital.

4 Dr Shock, as he came to be known, moved from the new South Africa to Canada, where he was charged in 2010 with sexually abusing a male patient.

5 Tony Peake is also a published novelist and biographer.

6 They were Ampie Coetzee, Ernst Liebenberg and John Miles, who were later joined by Gerrit Olivier.

7 Correctly called *Jacobsen's Index of Objectionable Literature*.

8 Others in the cast were: Blaise Koch, Timmy Kwebulana, André Lombard, Hannes Muller and Johann Myburgh.

9 Showground Road has now been renamed Enoch Sontonga, after the man who composed the South African national anthem.

10 Although the Afrikaans word 'speel' can mean both 'play' and 'act', there is little doubt what was meant here.

11 Anti-Apartheids Beweging Nederland.

12 *The Go-Between*, London: Hamish Hamilton, 1953.

13 Published by Nick Hern.

14 Theresa Edlmann, 'Division in the (Inner) Ranks'. Paper presented as part of the Rhodes History Dept Panel at the South African Historical Society Conference, UKZN, Durban 27-29 June 2011.

15 See Gary Baines 2009, 'Site of struggle: the Freedom Park fracas and the divisive legacy of South Africa's Border War/Liberation Struggle'. *Social Dynamics* 35(2): 330-344. Available at: DOI: 10.1080/02533950903076428 URL: dx.doi.org/10.1080/02533950903076428

REPUBLIC OF SOUTH AFRICA
GOVERNMENT GAZETTE
STAATSKOERANT
VAN DIE REPUBLIEK VAN SUID-AFRIKA

PRICE (GST included) 30c PRYS (AVB ingesluit)

Registered at the Post Office as a Newspaper   ABROAD 40c BUITELANDS   *As 'n Nuusblad by die Poskantoor Geregistreer*

POST FREE · POSVRY

Vol. 219   PRETORIA, 9 SEPTEMBER 1983   No. 8883

GOVERNMENT NOTICES

DEPARTMENT OF THE PRIME MINISTER

No. 2012   9 September 1983

APPOINTMENT OF ACTING MINISTER

It is hereby notified that the State President has appointed the Honourable D. W. Steyn, M.P., from 4 September 1983 as acting Minister of Community Development during the absence from the Republic of South Africa of the Honourable S. F. Kotzé, M.P.

DEPARTMENT OF INTERNAL AFFAIRS

No. 2016   9 September 1983

UNDESIRABLE PUBLICATIONS OR OBJECTS

A committee referred to in section 4 of the Publications Act, 1974, as amended, decided under section 11 (2) of the said Act that the undermentioned publications or objects are undesirable within the meaning of section 47 (2) of the said Act:

GOEWERMENTSKENNISGEWINGS

DEPARTEMENT VAN DIE EERSTE MINISTER

No. 2012   9 September 1983

AANSTELLING VAN WAARNEMENDE MINISTER

Hierby word bekendgemaak dat die Staatspresident Sy Edele D. W. Steyn, L.V., van 4 September 1983 af as waarnemende Minister van Gemeenskapsontwikkeling, aangestel het gedurende die afwesigheid uit die Republiek van Suid-Afrika van Sy Edele S. F. Kotzé, L.V.

DEPARTEMENT VAN BINNELANDSE AANGELEENTHEDE

No. 2016   9 September 1983

ONGEWENSTE PUBLIKASIES OF VOORWERPE

'n Komitee bedoel in artikel 4 van die Wet op Publikasies, 1974, soos gewysig, het kragtens artikel 11 (2) van genoemde Wet beslis dat die ondergenoemde publikasies of voorwerpe ongewens is binne die bedoeling van artikel 47 (2) van genoemde Wet:

LIST/LYS P83/85

Entry No. Inskrywing No.	Publication or object Publikasie of voorwerp	Author or producer Skrywer of voortbringer	Section 47 (2) Artikel 47 (2)
P83/8/14 .... P83/8/16	*Somewhere on the Border* (Play/Toneelteks) ...... *Go, Sell*—An investigation into the failure of the British Churches to meet the challenge of investment in apartheid	Anthony Akerman .... David Haslam	(a) + (e) (e)
P83/8/127	*Facts and Reports*—13th Vol, No P, August 5, '83	Edited by the Holland Committee on Southern Africa (Angola Comité), Amsterdam, Holland	(e)
P83/8/133	*Voice of the Youth: Islam and the P.C. Proposals* (Pamphlet/Pamflet)	Not stated/Nie vermeld nie	(e)
P83/8/134	*P.C. Proposals, The*—Reform or Repression?	Muslim Students Association—Natal Region (UNB, UND, UNP, UDW, SCE and Technikon)	(e)

Directorate of Publications,
Private Bag X9069,
Cape Town, 8000,
ZUID-AFRIKA.

13 May 1984.

RE: SOMEWHERE ON THE BORDER BY ANTHONY AKERMAN.

Dear Sir,

It has recently been brought to my attention that the above-mentioned play has been banned in South Africa. I am the author of the play which was staged in Holland under the auspices of Thekwini Theater in November 1983. According to the Government Gazette dated 9 September 1983, the play was banned under Section 47 (2), (a) + (e).

Please would you furnish me with the following information. Is the play still banned in South Africa? How was it possible to ban the play which had its first public performance on 8 November 1983 and was published on 11 November 1983? In effect the play didn't "exist" before then, so I would be very interested to hear your explanation. And, finally, I would appreciate it if you would provide me with a detailed list of all the offending passages in the script.

Yours faithfully,

Anthony Akerman,
Artistic Director.

Republiek van Suid-Afrika   Republic of South Africa

Telegramadres
Telegraphic address FILCEN

Tel. No. 45-6518

Direktoraat van Publikasies
Directorate of Publications
Privaatsak/Private Bag X9069
8000 KAAPSTAD/CAPE TOWN

Mr Anthony Akerman
Stichting Thekwini Theater
Post box 16949
1001 xr AMSTERDAM

Verw. No. P83/8/14
Ref. No. DP 3/17/4

1984-05-24

Dear Mr Akerman

PUBLICATIONS ACT, 1974 : PUBLICATION :
"SOMEWHERE ON THE BORDER"

Thank you for your letter of 13 May 1984.

The script of your play has been examined by a Committee of Publications on 5 September 1983 and was as correctly stated by you,
found to be undesirable within the meaning of section 47(2)(a) and
(e) of the Act. Section 47(2) reads as follows:

"For the purposes of this Act any publication or object, film,
public entertainment or intended public entertainment shall be
deemed to be undesirable if it or any part of it - (a) is in-
decent or obscene or is offensive or harmful to public morals;
(e) is prejudicial to the safety of the state, the general
welfare or the peace and good order."

The script was examined as a publication and not as a public entertainment and after examining the publication the statutory Committee of Publications gave the following reasons for their decision:

"The language used in the book is not only vulgar but will be
offensive to the reasonable and balanced reader and is there-
for undesirable within the meaning of section 47(2)(a) of the
Act. See the following, pages in brackets: fuck off (3),
cunt-eyed (3), arse (5), dumb cunt (7), shit (7), moer (8),
shit (8), I'll pull a cow's cunt over your heand and let a bull
fuck some sense into it (9), poeslap (18), jou gat (19), poephol (21), vuilgat (22), you want these cunts to shit blood (23),
balls (25), fart (25), kakstorie (32), fucken homo (32), Bors
uit, pens in, poephol opgeknoop (38), she just sucked in my
balls and spat out the pips (50), She opens her knees slightly
and you hear this soft sucking sound as the lips pull apart (66).

2/.....

Rig korrespondensie aan die Direkteur van Publikasies en nie aan ander individue nie.
Address correspondence to the Director of Publications and not to other individuals.

In the closing parts of the book the South African Armed Forces are placed in an extremely bad light and in this way it is undesirable within the meaning of section 47(2)(e) of the Act."

The script may not be distributed in the Republic of South Africa but a play could be staged if the parts which were found to be offensive are deleted.

Yours faithfully

DIRECTOR OF PUBLICATIONS

Directorate of Publications,
Private Bag X9069,
Cape Town, 8000,
ZUID-AFRIKA.

31 May 1984.

RE: "SOMEWHERE ON THE BORDER" BY ANTHONY AKERMAN.

Dear Sir,

Thank you for your letter of 24 May 1984, in which you defined the terms
under which my abovementioned play is banned in South Africa. It's
reassuring to know that by deleting the offending passages (words) you
cited, the play would be acceptable as a public entertainment.

There is one question, however, that remains unanswered and continues to
mystify me. I would like to know how the Board came to be in possession
of a script on 5 September 1983. As I mentioned in my last letter, the
play was published in the Netherlands on 11 November 1983. I notice that
the page numbering you quote corresponds with the typed rehearsal script
of the play. This was a script made for internal use only and was never
distributed publicly, and certainly not in South Africa. I did send one
of these scripts to my colleague, the playwright Athol Fugard, in June 1983
and he has subsequently told me that it never arrived. To the best of my
memory, this script also contains an inscribed dedication to the above-
mentioned author. Is this the script that came into the Board's possession?

Yours faithfully,

Anthony Akerman,
Artistic Director.

Republiek van Suid-Afrika Republic of South Africa

Telegramadres
Telegraphic address FILCEN

Tel. No. 45-6518

Direktoraat van Publikasies
Directorate of Publications
Privaatsak/Private Bag X9069
8000 KAAPSTAD/CAPE TOWN

•   •

Mr Anthony Akerman
Stichting Thekwini Theater
Post box 16949
1001 xr Amsterdam

Verw. No.   P83/8/14
Ref. No.   DP3/17/4

•   •

Dear Mr Akerman

PUBLICATIONS ACT, 1974 : PUBLICATION : SOMEWHERE
ON THE BORDER

I hereby wish to acknowledge receipt of your letter dated 31 May 1984.

The script of your play was submitted to the Directorate in accordance
with section 10 of the Publications Act which reads that any person
who desires to obtain a decision of a committee on the question whether
a publication is undesirable in the opinion of the committee shall
submit an application together with the publication to the Directorate.
The Directorate does not however disclose the name of the submitter.

Section 47(1)(xx) of the Publications Act defines a publication as
follows:-

   "(b)   any book, periodical, pamphlet, poster or other printed
          matter ...

    (c)   any writing or typescript which has in any manner been
          duplicated ..."

The script is unfortunately not in the Directorate's possession any
longer as it has been returned to the submitter. According to your
explanation the publication examined by the committee could well be a
script you made for internal use but this aspect is not taken into
account when a publication is examined. When the hundreds of publications which are submitted by various people comply with the defini-
tion of a publication as described in section 47(1)(xx), the Directorate submits them to committees for examination.

I hope that I have been of assistance to you.

Yours faithfully

DIRECTOR OF PUBLICATIONS

Rig korrespondensie aan die Direkteur van Publikasies en nie aan ander individue nie.
Address correspondence to the Director of Publications and not to other individuals.

Keep the letters rolling.
Glen Biderman-Pam (LEVITT)

Somewhere
on the Border

Cast

David Levitt
Black Actor
Trevor Mowbray
Bombardier Kotze
Hennie Badenhorst
Paul Marais
Doug Campbell

Somewhere on the Border was originally produced by Thekwini Theater and was first presented at Theater aan de Haven, The Hague, on 11 November 1983. The production was directed by Anthony Akerman, assisted by Anky Mager, with design and lighting by Apostolos Panagopoulos, costumes by Ena Heese and sound by Martin Cleaver.

DAVID LEVITT was played by Joss Levine, BLACK ACTOR by Joseph Mosikili, TREVOR MOWBRAY by Richard Carter, BOMBARDIER KOTZE by Peter Cartwright, HENNIE BADENHORST by Jeroen Kranenburg, PAUL MARAIS by Ian Bruce and DOUG CAMPBELL by Allan Leas.

In 2011 the play was revived for the National Arts Festival in Grahamstown, 25 years after the first South African production premiered there. The production was directed by André Odendaal with design and lighting by Kosie Smit. The stage manager was Joanna Borton.

DAVID LEVITT was played by Glen Biderman-Pam, BLACK ACTOR by Ndino Ndilula, TREVOR MOWBRAY by Kaz McFadden, BOMBARDIER KOTZE by Charles Bouguenon, HENNIE BADENHORST by André Lötter, PAUL MARAIS by Luan Jacobs and DOUG CAMPBELL by Dylan Horley.

The Time

The recent past.

The Setting

The play is set in a training camp somewhere in South Africa, in the operational area somewhere on the border between Namibia and Angola, and in the south of Angola.

Scene 1

A gate. Darkness. As the first strains of Jungle by the Electric Light Orchestra are heard, a subdued, nocturnal lighting is introduced. A lone sentry is on guard duty. It is LEVITT. *He wears Walkman headphones. As he walks across the stage a* BLACK ACTOR *wearing civilian clothes walks along behind him, draws an imaginary six shooter and guns him down, then crosses upstage through the gate.* LEVITT *pauses. He removes the headphones and the music stops. He looks around him.*

LEVITT: Halt! Who goes there? [*He peers into the audience.*] Is anyone there?

He replaces the headphones and we immediately hear the music again. He begins 'composing' a letter.

Dearest Sharon. No. Darling Sharon. My dearest, darling Sharon. Howzit? I miss you stacks. Man, I'm sorry I couldn't work a pass this weekend. Please try and understand. I only got one letter from you this week. What's going on? [*Realising this sounds like a complaint he corrects himself.*] No …

Pause.

Please try and understand. Keep the letters rolling, Sharon! I'll try and write every day. I think of you all the time. Where are you tonight? Are you going to Gavin's party anyway? Did that Stan Rabinowitz ask you? Just remember, Sharon, he's only after one thing and he'll have no respect for you after. Don't do it, Sharon. I need you, man. Remember I'm faithful to you, hey. I know I haven't got much choice here, but still. Fair is fair, hey. Ja, I know you get lonely, but try and see it my way. As long as I got you, Sharon, they can't break me. There's talk of us maybe going up to the border. Can you wait that long for me, Sharon? Well, spans of love. Your Dave. H O L L A N D. Hope Our Love Lives And Never Dies. [*He lights a cigarette.*]
S I A M. Sexual Intercourse At Midnight.

MOWBRAY *appears upstage and advances silently towards* LEVITT. *He plucks the cigarette from* Levitt's *lips.*

MOWBRAY: What's this, hey?
LEVITT: Hi there, Trev.
MOWBRAY: What's this? I'm asking.
LEVITT: What's the problem?
MOWBRAY: This! To my face you say you got no skyfs [smokes] and then behind my back you come here to zoll on your ace [smoke on your own].

MOWBRAY *takes a drag and blows smoke in* Levitt's *face.*

LEVITT: I only had one left, man.
MOWBRAY: Is it?
LEVITT: As a matter of fact, ja.

MOWBRAY: You act like I'm your china and then you come sideways at me like a crab.

LEVITT: You want to see the packet?

MOWBRAY: Ag, fuck off to Israel.

LEVITT: Take my oath.

MOWBRAY: You lie like your feet stink, Levitt.

LEVITT: Give me my smoke back.

As LEVITT *reaches for the cigarette,* MOWBRAY *makes stabbing gestures towards him with the glowing end.*

MOWBRAY: I burn you.

LEVITT: Pull out, man.

MOWBRAY: You sukkel with me [you mess with me], I kill you dead.

LEVITT: Don't be pathetic.

MOWBRAY: Cunt-eyed schmo of a typical Jewboy.

LEVITT: Look, cut it out.

MOWBRAY: Make me.

LEVITT: Just grow up.

MOWBRAY: Voetsek! [*He gives* LEVITT *a push. Upstage we can discern the figure of* KOTZE.]

I don't like you. It's not personal. I just hate Jews.

LEVITT: Take that back.

MOWBRAY: Here [Jesus], I'll thump you, Levitt.

LEVITT: Take it back!

MOWBRAY: You sailing for a nailing, Jewboy.

LEVITT: You making me lose my temper.

MOWBRAY: I gob in your face. [*He shows* LEVITT *a ball of spit on the end of his tongue.*]

I land this greenie right on your Jewboy nose.

LEVITT: You forcing me to … [MOWBRAY *spits in* Levitt's *face.* LEVITT *lashes out at him. They end up on the ground with* LEVITT *on top.*]

You asked for it.

KOTZE *moves towards them.*

KOTZE: Aandag [attention]! [MOWBRAY *and* LEVITT *scramble to their feet and stand to attention.*] I come here to inspect the guard and I find you behaving like a pair of moffies [queers]. Come here!

KOTZE *takes each by an earlobe and knocks their heads together.*

Look out there. What you see? You see South Africa. What else? Blackness. Die Swart Gevaar [The Black Peril]. You here to watch that, not to play silly buggers. Watch it! It's black and dangerous.

Blackout.

This is called a troublemaker.

Dylan Horley (CAMPBELL), Kaz McFadden (MOWBRAY),
Charles Bouguenon (KOTZE), Glen Biderman-Pam (LEVITT),
André Lötter (BADENHORST) and Luan Jacobs (MARAIS).

Scene 2

The bungalow. Rows of iron beds on either side of a central walkway. Early morning. MARAIS and BADENHORST are still in their sleeping bags on top of beds already made up for inspection. BADENHORST stirs, looks into the sleeping bag and addresses his member.

BADENHORST: Hey, behave yourself!

MARAIS *wakes up with a shout.*

What's your case?

MARAIS: Klein Klaas, you know, he was running down there by the cement dam. He's the boy on the farm. And, no, ja, wait, I was under the bluegums. You know, just sitting.

BADENHORST: Give your mouth a chance, Paul.

MARAIS: He was running there with his knees bent, carrying two buckets and they almost touched the dirt. Then he came there on the wall of the dam. It was Klein Klaas. Suddenly he klaps up [slaps up] into the air and falls slowly over into the water. Like a film. Then I heard this shot, Hennie. I got such a skrik [fright] I jumped, man. I tried to run there, but my legs went all slap [weak] and I fell down. Oubaas Venter said: Leave it, Paul. He was going to poison the water. I could smell the oil from his rifle. Klein Klaas was floating and there was all blood. I was then on the wall and he says: Why do you shoot me, Baas Paul? And I can't say nothing. I'm all sticky from blood. I try to catch him with my hands, but he's got no hands. Just stumps that slip. And he's saying: Why? Why? Why?

BADENHORST: 'Cause Y's a crooked letter and you can't make it straight.

MARAIS: How late is it?

BADENHORST: Too late, she cried.

KOTZE (*off*): Move, you dumb cunt!

CAMPBELL, *wearing civilian clothing and laden down with army kit, enters. He is followed by* KOTZE.

MARAIS: Aandag!

MARAIS *and* BADENHORST *jump to attention.*

KOTZE: Here God, wat die fok gaan hier aan? [Jesus God, what the fuck is going on here?] You cunts is asking for shit, nè? This place looks like a whore's handbag. I try and treat you like white men and look what happens. Slaan die dek! [Hit the deck!]

MARAIS *and* BADENHORST *get down and start doing press-ups.* KOTZE *turns to* CAMPBELL.

Moenie vir my loer nie, ek is nie 'n hoer nie. Weet jy wat jy is, Engelsman? Jy's 'n urk. Weet jy wat 'n urk is? 'n Urk is 'n dinges wat in jou gat in kruip en gedurende die nag sluip hy na buite en blaf vir jou ballas. Verstaan jy? [Don't stare at me. I'm not a whore. Do you know what you are, Englishman? You're an urk. Do you know what an urk is? An urk is a thing that crawls up your arse and at night it creeps out and barks at your balls. You understand?]

CAMPBELL: Could you repeat that in English, please Bombardier?

KOTZE: Jou ma se moer. [Go and fuck yourself.] You see how these men are shitting off, Kammel? You know why, Kammel? It's because you are full of shit, Kammel.

CAMPBELL: My name's Campbell, Bombardier.

KOTZE: Is that so?

CAMPBELL: Yes, Bombardier.

KOTZE: Wrong, Kammel! I tell you what is your name.

CAMPBELL: My name's Campbell, Bombardier.

KOTZE: Listen, my man, I'm going to tell you something. [*To the others.*] You sound like a bunch of women on the job. On your feet! Now look at this rubbish here. This is called a troublemaker. He's no trouble to me, but he's going to make trouble for you. I'm going to tell you something, Kammel, so you better listen good. You perhaps think you a big deal. But take it from me, I'm not impressed. I can eat ten of your kind before breakfast, Kammel. I'm a hard man. I take my holidays on the Caprivi Strip. I've broken men twice your size. I've heard them cry out for their mothers, Kammel. So if you coming here thinking the sun shines out your arse, you got two chances: no chance and fuck-all chance. That's not a joke, Kammel! I don't make jokes. I straighten people out. And if you don't get into line, I'll pull a cow's cunt over your head and let a bull fuck some sense into it. You understand what I'm talking, Kammel?

CAMPBELL: Yes, Bombardier.

KOTZE: You say something, Kammel?

CAMPBELL: Yes, Bombardier.

KOTZE: What was that?

CAMPBELL: Yes, Bombardier!!!

KOTZE: I hope you not pulling my legs. Right! You lot thought you had a free Saturday. That's what comes from thinking. Full-kit inspection at 1700 hours. I want to see how our troublemaker settles in. And this place better shine. Right?

ALL: Yes, Bombardier.

KOTZE: What?

ALL: Yes, Bombardier!!!

KOTZE: Who's got a driving licence around here?

BADENHORST: Me, Bombardier!

KOTZE: Put on some clothes, get up to the NCO [non-commissioned officer] mess on the double and wash my car.

BADENHORST *groans and starts getting dressed.*

Get your things packed out, Kammel. And get rid of those moffie clothes. You'll probably never wear civvies again. Is jy al daar [are you there yet], Badenhorst?

KOTZE *marches off briskly, followed by* BADENHORST. MARAIS *crosses to* CAMPBELL.

MARAIS: I'm Paul Marais.
CAMPBELL: Oh.

MARAIS *shakes his hand.*

Ja, Campbell. Doug.
MARAIS: Doug?
CAMPBELL: Campbell.
MARAIS: So. How goes it?
CAMPBELL: Does the larney [white boss] always lay on the heavy vibes?
MARAIS: Excuse me?
CAMPBELL: The Bombardier.
MARAIS: Kotze?
CAMPBELL: Does he always go apeshit?
MARAIS: No, on the moment he seems a bit omgekrap [upset].
CAMPBELL: Truly!
MARAIS: But if we pull together, then he's white.
CAMPBELL: Hey, well.
MARAIS: Have you been in some trouble?
CAMPBELL: Can you lend us some goeters [stuff] to clean this shit?
MARAIS: No fine.

MARAIS *gives* CAMPBELL *a cleaning kit.*

What camp do you come from?
CAMPBELL: Pretoria.
MARAIS: You weren't in the DB [detention barracks] there?
CAMPBELL: Naught.
MARAIS: I just thought …
CAMPBELL: For sure.

An awkward pause.

MARAIS: I think I'll perhaps go help Hennie with the car.
CAMPBELL: Safe.
MARAIS: Excuse me?
CAMPBELL: No, I'll sight you then.
MARAIS: No fine, Doug. Just make yourself at home, hey.

MARAIS *leaves.* CAMPBELL *takes in his new surroundings.*

Blackout.

We hear a message on a radio request programme for national servicemen.

And here's a card now and it goes to Corporal Brian Adams, somewhere on the border. We're praying and thinking of him daily and we pray the time will pass speedily and we pray for his safe return. And we're also thinking of all the fellows with him in C Company. And it comes from Mum, Dad, Sean and sister Desiré. That's to Corporal Brian Adams, somewhere on the border. I do hope, Brian, that you heard the message ...

What colour is this, Kammel?

Dylan Horley (CAMPBELL), Kaz McFadden (MOWBRAY)
and Charles Bouguenon (KOTZE).

Scene 3

Lights up on the bungalow as CAMPBELL *lights a cigarette.*
LEVITT *lays out* CAMPBELL*'s kit for inspection. He walks on
taxis, small squares of blanket used to polish the floor as he shuffles
around. The sound now comes from Levitt's radio. The message is
followed by commercial jingles.* CAMPBELL *turns it off. He pays
no attention to* LEVITT.

LEVITT: Then you just square off your bed with your dixies [army
    mess kit] … so. Here the towel at the bottom and on that you put
    the moving parts of your rifle, your Bible, your razor and other
    stuff, like that see? Hey, are you watching?

CAMPBELL: What?

LEVITT: I'm not catching a thrill here.

CAMPBELL: What's cutting you?

LEVITT: Next time you'll have to do it yourself.

CAMPBELL: For sure.

LEVITT: Look, if you're still in civvies at inspection we'll all shit
    off.

CAMPBELL [*holding up a pair of trousers and a shirt*]: There's it
    now.

LEVITT: Ja. Browns, pairs one, wearing for the use of. In two sizes:
    too big and too small.

CAMPBELL: Hey, but true, ek sê [I say].

LEVITT: How come they sent you to our regiment so late?

CAMPBELL: I been here and there.

LEVITT: You weren't RTU-ed [returned to unit] from the parabats
    or something?

CAMPBELL: Are you serious?

LEVITT: No, it's just that this other ou [guy], Mowbray, he was.

CAMPBELL: Truly.

LEVITT: Where you been then?

CAMPBELL: That's another story again. Like I wasn't really into making choices, but come my call up I put in a no-show.

LEVITT: I wasn't stoked about doing my army either, but what can a ou do?

CAMPBELL: For sure.

LEVITT: They got us by the short and curlies.

CAMPBELL: Well, like the trick is: don't let yourself get taken within yourself. You know what I mean like?

LEVITT: Sort of.

CAMPBELL: Some Russian cat once said: 'To live is to burn.' And me, I was into burning. I flashed on this idea: I'm going to see the country. I needed space, so I hit out.

CAMPBELL *puts the cigarette out on the floor. He starts changing into his army uniform.* LEVITT *picks up the cigarette end.*

It was a radical buzz. I had no bread, didn't graft, just lived off the land. Hey, I could really dig the beauty of the country. I tell you what, the energy out there is unreal. Some of the most amazing cats I met were black. Like I could really get into their philosophy of life. Hey, this one cat, Amos! We'd just bust a bottleneck [smoked dagga using the neck of the bottle as a pipe] together. The sun was like setting and we were taking hits, and then I got this full-on rush. This is Africa! Like we were so close and digging each other's company, the future could have started then. I found peace, ek sê. [*By this time he has changed. He looks at himself in his army uniform.*] And now I'm doing my army. Will that pass inspection?

LEVITT: Search me. Kotze's a mad bastard and with him, you know, you never know.

CAMPBELL: Has like anything been said to you cats about going to the border?

LEVITT: Rumours. But you never know what to believe.

CAMPBELL: Hey, well.

LEVITT: If they post us up on border duty, ja, I don't know. Already I miss my cherry a stack. And you can't really, you know, expect them to be faithful, but still.

CAMPBELL: For sure.

LEVITT: Do you want to see a picture of her? [*He immediately produces a photograph from his wallet.*]
That's Sharon.

CAMPBELL: Hey, then.

LEVITT: I really smaak her a stack [like her a lot]. Sometimes I think it would drive me mad if she, you know.

CAMPBELL: Hey, ek sê, don't tune that.

LEVITT: Anyway.

CAMPBELL: Find the power within yourself.

LEVITT: Ja, vasbyt [hang in there], I suppose.

CAMPBELL: You know then.

CAMPBELL *sits on his bed in the lotus position and closes his eyes.*

LEVITT: Not on the bed! I just made the creases.

BADENHORST *and* MARAIS *enter.*

BADENHORST: Are the Jews and the communists getting together? Take a joke, Davy my maat [my friend]. [*He stops in front of Campbell's bed.*]
Well I'll be buggered. What's his story?

LEVITT: I think he's meditating.

BADENHORST: Paul, come and look at this, man.

MARAIS: What's that?

LEVITT: Thinking to yourself.

BADENHORST: If he drops us in shit at inspection, I'll give him something to think about.

MARAIS: He seems like a good ou.

BADENHORST: How do you know?

MARAIS: We had a talk this morning.

BADENHORST: Well, if the Bombardier comes past and he's sitting there on his bed like a coolie, we'll all shit through the eye of a needle.

They all start laying out their kit in silence. BADENHORST *keeps looking in Campbell's direction.*

This is now working on my nerves. Engelsman! The kaffirs are coming!

He starts bouncing Campbell's bed.

Stand up and fight for your country!

CAMPBELL: Don't give me that.

BADENHORST: Don't you want to fight for your country?

CAMPBELL: Go and swing in a tree.

BADENHORST: Are you a pacifist or a patriot?

MOWBRAY *enters.*

CAMPBELL: Get lost, apeman.

MOWBRAY: You talking to me?

BADENHORST: We got a troublemaker here.

MOWBRAY: You going to kill him dead?

MARAIS: Los him out, Hennie.

LEVITT: Get ready for inspection, man.

MOWBRAY: Don't give me a thousand words, Jewboy.

MARAIS: No, he's right.

All, except MOWBRAY *and* CAMPBELL *apply themselves to their kit.*

MOWBRAY: I don't gotta stand no bladdy inspection.

BADENHORST: Do something to your bed, Mowbray, it looks like a used poeslap [cunt rag].

MOWBRAY: Don't tune me grief.

MARAIS: Ag, Trevor, just pull together, man.

MOWBRAY: Don't give me uphill.

BADENHORST: Jy sal jou gat sien. [You'll see your arse.]

MOWBRAY: Fuck you! It's a free country. [*He crosses to* CAMPBELL.]

Howzit now, china?

CAMPBELL: Sweet. Yourself?

MOWBRAY: Crazy like a daisy. Could you see your way clear to borrowing me the lend of a smoke?

CAMPBELL: Safe.

CAMPBELL *hands* MOWBRAY *a packet of cigarettes. He takes one.*

MOWBRAY: Send it! Hennie, could I talk you into a coffin nail?

He throws the packet to BADENHORST.

BADENHORST: You could twist my arm.

BADENHORST *takes a cigarette, crushes it in his hand and lets the remains fall to the floor.*

CAMPBELL: That's really intelligent.

BADENHORST: Trevor, I can't interest you in a cigarette?

He throws the packet back to MOWBRAY, *who puts a few more cigarettes between his lips.* CAMPBELL *moves towards* MOWBRAY.

CAMPBELL: Hey china, we've all had a laugh now.

MOWBRAY: Is it?

MOWBRAY *throws the cigarettes to* BADENHORST. CAMPBELL *lunges in that direction, but is not fast enough. The packet is thrown back and forth, with* CAMPBELL *in pursuit.*

Moet ek bid vir 'n weerligstraal? [Must I pray for a flash of lightning?]

19

CAMPBELL *blocks the trajectory between* BADENHORST *and* MOWBRAY. BADENHORST *throws the cigarettes to* MARAIS, *who gives them to* CAMPBELL.

CAMPBELL: Thank you.

MOWBRAY, *with his back to the doorway, lights a match and holds it aloft.*

MOWBRAY: Brand, bliksem, brand! Die enigste hoop in donker Afrika! [Burn, lightning, burn! The only hope in darkest Africa!]

As he lights up KOTZE *appears in the doorway.*

MARAIS: Aandag!

The men dash for their beds and come to attention. MOWBRAY *conceals the cigarette in a cupped hand.*

KOTZE: Septic. [*He looks at them in silence.*]
Staan stil! [Stand still!] You at the end there with a face. You smoking?
MOWBRAY: No, Bombardier.
KOTZE: You calling me a liar?
MOWBRAY: No, Bombardier.
KOTZE: Hold out your hand. The other one, bokdrol [goat turd]! Now make a fist. And open it.

MOWBRAY *follows the instructions. The crushed and extinguished cigarette falls to the floor.* KOTZE *paces down the walkway leaving a trail of muddy footprints.*

For crying out loud, just look at that floor. You think you can take chances with me. But you wrong. I was in uniform when you was in liquid form.

KOTZE *puts on a white glove and begins the inspection. First Marais's kit, which seems spotless. He runs a finger under the bed frame and shows* MARAIS *the dirt on his glove. He moves to Badenhorst's bed and retrieves the remains of Campbell's crushed cigarette from the floor.*

This is not a kafferhok [kaffir cage], Badenhorst. What would your mother say to this?

BADENHORST: I don't know, Bombardier.

KOTZE: Well I do, poephol [arse hole]. Nothing! She would just weep from pity.

He looks long and hard at Mowbray's bed. He turns away. As he does so, he swings around and knocks MOWBRAY *sprawling. He stands in front of* CAMPBELL *making eye contact.*

Did you see me hit this man, Badenhorst?

BADENHORST: No, Bombardier.

KOTZE: What happened, Badenhorst?

BADENHORST: He fell over, Bombardier.

KOTZE: On your feet, vuilgat [dirty swine].

MOWBRAY *gets to his feet.* KOTZE *moves to Levitt's kit.*

For crying in a bucket. You try hard, Levitt, I'll give you that. But most of all you try your luck. You call this clean? Where's the love, man? What happened to your manly pride?

He scatters Levitt's kit about, then goes on to CAMPBELL. *He takes a piece of cotton wool from his pocket and rubs it on Campbell's cheek, leaving wisps clinging to his face.*

Trying to grow a beard, Kammel?

CAMPBELL: No, Bombardier.

KOTZE: Then what's this? Kammel, there's a war on the go. People is laying down their life for your freedom and you don't take the effort to shave. You letting down the whole side. Don't you care, man?

CAMPBELL: Not really, Bombardier.

KOTZE: What you say? You want these cunts to shit blood? Vat julle gewere! [Get your rifles!]

The others take their R1 rifles, hold them horizontally with outstretched arms and start turning.

You lower than shark shit, Kammel. So don't try and put yourself on my level.

CAMPBELL: I won't, Bombardier.

KOTZE: You think you different. But it's us against them, Kammel, and you on our side if you like it or not.

CAMPBELL: That's not what I believe, Bombardier.

KOTZE *takes a fold of loose skin on Campbell's hand between his thumb and forefinger and starts twisting.*

KOTZE: What colour is this, Kammel?

CAMPBELL *falls to his knees.*

What colour, you cunt? What colour?

CAMPBELL: Aaargh, white. White!

KOTZE: And don't you forget it.

CAMPBELL [*very softly*]: Fuck you!

KOTZE: What you say?

CAMPBELL: Nothing.

KOTZE *brings his face close to* Campbell's. *He taps his chin with his index finger.*

KOTZE: You want to try me, Kammel? Here, you want to hit me?

Pause.

I tell you something, Kammel. I fuck your mother. Her cunt's so big I have to push my fist in. But that's still not enough, so I push my head in. And what do I see? Roy Rogers! Hey Roy, I say, what you doing here? No man, he says, I'm just looking for my horse. But if you think I'm talking about a big cunt, you better find a mirror and take a look at yourself.

To the others.

Put down those rifles. I told you a troublemaker would only make trouble for you. All weekend passes is cancelled. You know who to thank for that? You know who?

ALL: Campbell.

KOTZE: Who?

ALL: Kammel!

KOTZE: Who?

ALL: Kammel!!!

KOTZE *marches off briskly. As* CAMPBELL *makes a move to get up the others put down their rifles and start moving towards him.*

BADENHORST: Get the bugger.

MOWBRAY: He'll pay for this.

MOWBRAY, MARAIS *and* BADENHORST *grab* CAMPBELL. *He struggles, but is powerless against these odds. They strip off his trousers and spread-eagle him across a steel trunk in the middle of the walkway.*

BADENHORST: Levitt, give us some polish.

LEVITT *remains seated.* BADENHORST *goes to his bed and gets a tin of shoe polish and a rag.*

CAMPBELL: Bloody fascists!

BADENHORST [*standing over* Campbell*'s face*]: Shut up or I fart in your face.

BADENHORST *smears polish on* Campbell's *balls. When the job is done, they release him and stand back.* CAMPBELL *stands and pulls up his trousers.*

Blackout.

If he drops us in shit at inspection, I'll give him something to think about.

Dylan Horley (CAMPBELL), André Lötter (BADENHORST)
and Glen Biderman-Pam (LEVITT).

Scene 4

The bungalow. CAMPBELL *is on his bed in the lotus position. There is a timid knock at the door. The* BLACK ACTOR, *wearing overalls, stands in the doorway. He knocks a second time before* CAMPBELL *notices him.*

BLACK ACTOR: Baas?
CAMPBELL: Yes?
BLACK ACTOR: Sorry, Baas.
CAMPBELL: What?
BLACK ACTOR: I'm bring that drinks, Baas.

He produces a bottle wrapped in brown paper.

CAMPBELL: For me?
BLACK ACTOR: No, Baas. I must bring it for the other baas.
CAMPBELL: Hey, well.
BLACK ACTOR: Where he is, the other baas?
CAMPBELL *shrugs.*
    What I must do?
CAMPBELL: Wait for him. [He *crosses to the* BLACK ACTOR.]
    Sit down and wait.
BLACK ACTOR: I'm better to stand.
CAMPBELL: What's the big deal? Sit down, man.

The BLACK ACTOR *sits reluctantly.*

    Want a smoke?

The BLACK ACTOR *gets up again and crosses to* CAMPBELL.

BLACK ACTOR: Thank you very much, Baas.
CAMPBELL: Hey man, I'm not a baas. My name's Doug.
BLACK ACTOR: Yes, Baas Doug.

CAMPBELL *offers him a light, but the* BLACK ACTOR *has already put the cigarette in his pocket.*

CAMPBELL: Do you work for the army?
BLACK ACTOR: Yes. I'm work some garden jobs. Yes.
CAMPBELL: Do you like the army?
BLACK ACTOR: Yes.
CAMPBELL: You're joking.
BLACK ACTOR: Yes.
CAMPBELL: The army's up to shit.
BLACK ACTOR: Yes.

BADENHORST *and* MOWBRAY *enter.* MOWBRAY *carries a family-size Coke.*

MOWBRAY: Hey houtkop [blockhead], what you fucken doing inside? This is not a bladdy kafferhok this.
BLACK ACTOR: I'm bring that drinks, Baas.

MOWBRAY *takes the* BLACK ACTOR'*s hat off and throws it on the floor.* CAMPBELL *retrieves it.*

BADENHORST: Come here, John. Why you take so bloody long, you lazy bastard?
BLACK ACTOR: I'm run there and back, Baas.
BADENHORST: I know you people.
BLACK ACTOR: I'm wait there long, long time by the Off Sales.
BADENHORST: You mean you were having a bhebha [fuck] in the bushes with one of your kaffir girls.
BLACK ACTOR: No, Baas. The baas, he was close the Off Sales for one hour. He is telling me to wait.
BADENHORST: You people always got a excuse. Come on, give here. Where's the change? Hurry up, chop, chop. What's this? Why's this short? Twenty rands take away fifteen rands sixty-nine is ...
BLACK ACTOR: Four rands thirty-one.

BADENHORST: You give me back three eighty-one.

BLACK ACTOR: The baas by the shop, he's give me that.

BADENHORST: You people can't be trusted.

BLACK ACTOR: No, Baas, I'm telling you. He's give me that.

BADENHORST: And here, from the goodness of my heart, I was thinking of giving you a tip.

BLACK ACTOR: Baas Bitzer, he's give me short.

BADENHORST: I tell you what. Go back and ask him that money. That's your tip.

BLACK ACTOR: He's never give me.

BADENHORST: That's your problem.

BLACK ACTOR: He's say I'm lie.

BADENHORST: That's your indaba [business].

BLACK ACTOR: My children, they hungry.

BADENHORST: I've heard that sob story before.

BLACK ACTOR: My wife, she is sick.

BADENHORST: Look, just don't come here crying to me.

BLACK ACTOR: How I must buy food?

BADENHORST: Sis, man, you smell. When did you wash? You mustn't come here smelling like that. Go wash. Come back and ask nicely. Then you see this fifty cent? You can have it.

CAMPBELL *grabs the coin from* BADENHORST *and gives it to the* BLACK ACTOR.

CAMPBELL: Here friend, it's yours.

BADENHORST: Fucking hell! Give here, John.

CAMPBELL: Don't listen to him. It's yours.

BADENHORST: Give here or I'll kick your bloody arse.

BLACK ACTOR: What I must do?

BADENHORST *moves towards the* BLACK ACTOR. CAMPBELL *steps between them.*

BADENHORST: You cheeky bastard!

CAMPBELL: Go! Get out of here.

BADENHORST: I'm warning you, John. For the last time.

BADENHORST *holds out his hand. The* BLACK ACTOR *is about to hand over the money.*

CAMPBELL: Don't be stupid! [*Pushes him out of the door.*]
Take it! Get the hell out of here.

BADENHORST: What you trying to prove?

CAMPBELL: What's it to you?

MOWBRAY: He's a kaffir-lover.

MOWBRAY *sets up the drinks in enamel mugs on a steel trunk.*

BADENHORST: He doesn't know what you talking about, Trevor.

MOWBRAY: Is it?

BADENHORST: No, when he's around you must say: 'black person'.

MOWBRAY: Well, I could of sworn it was a kaffir.

MARAIS *and* LEVITT *enter.*

BADENHORST: Hey, you ous, come and steek 'n dop [have a drink].

MOWBRAY: Cane for the pain!

MARAIS: I'm sorry, Doug. I just went blank.

CAMPBELL: Leave it.

BADENHORST: Bring your arse to anchor, Paul.

BADENHORST *and* MOWBRAY *have embarked on some serious drinking.* LEVITT *and* MARAIS *join them.*

MOWBRAY: Hey, black-person lover, you want to drink with the main manne [men]?

CAMPBELL *doesn't respond.*

What's his case?

BADENHORST: He's having his period.

MARAIS: Los [leave] him out, Hennie.

BADENHORST: That reminds me. And I'm not pulling your leg, hey Kammel. There was this ou – wife, kids, steady job, the lot. Anyway he wakes up one morning, looks under the sheets and what does he see?

MARAIS: What?

BADENHORST: His balls has turned brown. No, joking apart and present company excepted, hey Kammel. You can imagine, he gets a moerava [very big] fright. So he phones this doctor and goes around to see him quick sticks. Well he's in there, rods round his ankles, and the doc's checking out his balls.

MOWBRAY: Fucken homo.

BADENHORST: No serious. But the doctor's stumped. He doesn't know where it comes from. So he says, 'no listen, I can't put my finger on it right now, but here's some pills what might help'. So this ou drinks some pills and nothing happens. Days go by. He drinks all the pills, but still his balls stay brown. Now he's really down in the dumps and he's getting helluva frustrated. Anyway he goes home one day and there he slips on some toys on the lounge floor and that finally strips his moer [makes him lose his temper]. So he starts shouting the wife out. 'I'm out working my fingers to the bone to make our living and you let the place here go to rack and ruin, toys laying around, the works.' But the wife's also been having a hard time, so she starts howling and says, 'ja you do fuck all in the home and I've got to look after the kids and they been sick, and the pipe in the bathroom's burst, and the sink's blocked. I don't even have time to wipe my arse. I know, says the ou, that's another thing I want to talk to you about.'

All, except CAMPBELL, *have a good laugh.*

CAMPBELL: You trying to say something?

31

MOWBRAY: Go gently like a Bentley.

CAMPBELL: I wasn't talking to you. I was talking to the plank with the sense of humour.

BADENHORST: Go fuck spiders, party-pooper.

CAMPBELL: You shouldn't drink if you can't handle it.

CAMPBELL *picks up the bottle of cane, takes a mouthful, which he doesn't swallow, then pours the rest over the steel trunk.*

MOWBRAY: Kill him!

BADENHORST: Now you going to come short.

BADENHORST *moves towards* CAMPBELL.

LEVITT: Break it up, you ous.

MOWBRAY: Dip his lights, Hennie.

BADENHORST *delivers a roundhouse punch, which* CAMPBELL *ducks.* CAMPBELL *spits the cane in* BADENHORST's *eyes. As* BADENHORST's *hands go to his face* CAMPBELL *kicks him in the balls.* BADENHORST *doubles up holding his balls and* CAMPBELL *knocks him to the ground.*

CAMPBELL: Okay. Okay.

BADENHORST *gets up slowly.*

MARAIS: Enough is enough.

LEVITT: Make friends now.

CAMPBELL: I don't want to fight.

BADENHORST: Now you going to suffer, little man.

CAMPBELL: Hey, let's leave it.

BADENHORST: You going to die.

MOWBRAY [*throwing a webbing belt to* BADENHORST]: Here, Hennie.

BADENHORST *lashes out at* CAMPBELL *with the belt.* MARAIS *jumps in and takes the belt away from him.*

MARAIS: No, that's not right.

BADENHORST: Then I take him apart with my bare hands.

LEVITT: What you trying to prove, Hennie?

BADENHORST: Just who's a man around here.

He lunges towards CAMPBELL*, who sidesteps and trips him. He lands on the floor and* CAMPBELL *kicks him in the stomach.* MARAIS *goes to* BADENHORST.

MARAIS: You all right, Hennie?

BADENHORST: No, I'm all right. I just tripped. It's the drink, man.

LEVITT: Call it quits now.

MOWBRAY: You ous fought like men. It was just like in the Bats. But now you must be friends, hey. Shake on it.

CAMPBELL *and* BADENHORST *shake hands. They squeeze hard and only let go when* MOWBRAY *has finished talking.*

I say one thing about the army. Just one thing. You the best fucken mates to have. Swear to God. We go through the shit together. Through thick and thin shit. And that makes us chinas for life.

BADENHORST: Okay Doug, you heard the man.

CAMPBELL: Safe.

CAMPBELL *looks at his hand.*

BADENHORST: What's that?

CAMPBELL: Blood.

They look at each other and start laughing.

Blackout.

Levitt!! In Hitler's day we would have made soap out of you.

Dylan Horley (CAMPBELL), Kaz McFadden (MOWBRAY),
André Lötter (BADENHORST), Glen Biderman-Pam (LEVITT),
Luan Jacobs (MARAIS), Charles Bouguenon (KOTZE) and
Ndino Ndilula (BLACK ACTOR).

Scene 5

A parade ground. Sunlight. Rising above the laughter of the previous scene is the voice of the BLACK ACTOR singing a freedom song. He enters, carrying a sack filled with sawdust. His singing is drowned by the sound of approaching soldiers. He takes up a position near the audience and ad libs a humorous commentary on what follows.

KOTZE [*off*]: Hik-hak, hik-hak, hik-hak, yuugh; hik-hak, hik-hak, hik-hak, yuugh; hik-hak, hik-hak, hik-hak, hik-hak, yuugh.

The soldiers march towards the audience at an insane pace.

Markeer die pas! [Mark time!] Hik-hak, hik-hak, hik-hak, yuugh! Levitt!! In Hitler's day we would have made soap out of you! Hik-hak, hik-hak, hik-hak, yuugh; hik-hak, hik-hak, hik-hak, yuugh; hik-hak, hik-hak, hik-hak, yuugh. Halt! Dat klink soos boontjies in 'n pispot. Julle wil nie saamwerk nie. Julle sê fok jou, Bombardier. Goed, ons gaan aan. [That sounds like beans in a pisspot. You don't want to work together. You say, fuck you, Bombardier. Fine, we'll carry on.] Markeer die pas! Hik-hak, hik-hak, hik-hak, yuugh. Tel daardie vuile pote op! [Pick up those dirty feet!] Parallel to the ground! Hik-hak, hik-hak, hik-hak, yuugh.

He makes them mark time for a long while; the theatre is filled with the sound of pounding boots.

Halt! Mowbray!! If you ever out of time again I'll put your cock in your arse and carry you down to the station like a suitcase. Regs om! [Right turn!] Count the fucking time. Links om! [Left turn!]

ALL: Een, twee-drie, een! [One, two-three, one!]

KOTZE: Omkeer! [About turn!]

ALL: Een, twee-drie, een.

KOTZE *marches them upstage and gives them rifle drill.*

KOTZE: Kammel, you cunt, I'll climb down your throat and shit on your heart. Op die plek rus! [Stand at ease!] Kammel, kom hier! [Come here!]

CAMPBELL *falls out of the platoon and halts in front of* KOTZE.

You see that tree over there? Go fetch me a leaf. Is jy al terug? [Are you back yet?]

CAMPBELL *runs off. The* BLACK ACTOR *is laughing and doing a send-up of* KOTZE.

Kaffer! Wat soek jy? [What do you want?]

BLACK ACTOR: Oh shit. Baas? Ekskies Baas? [Excuse me, boss?]

KOTZE: Kom hier, dom donder. [Come here, you stupid fool.]

The BLACK ACTOR *comes to attention in front of* KOTZE *and salutes him.*

BLACK ACTOR: Ja Baas?

KOTZE: Jy moenie kak droog maak nie, kaffer. [You mustn't cause shit, kaffir.]

BLACK ACTOR: Nee Baas. Maar die Grootbaas het gesê dat ek daardie dinges in die andere dinges in moes hang. [No boss. But the big boss said that I have to hang that thing in the other thing.]

KOTZE: Watter Grootbaas? [What big boss?]

BLACK ACTOR: Ek weet nie sy naam nie. Hulle lyk almal dieselfde. [I don't know his name. They all look the same.]

KOTZE: Kakstorie, kaffer. [Shit story, kaffir.]

CAMPBELL *runs on. He halts in front of* KOTZE *and presents him*

36

with a leaf.

You trying to play stupid with me, Kammel? What's this, hey?

CAMPBELL: It's a leaf, Bombardier.

KOTZE: Sê vir my kaffer, hierdie is seker nie die regte blaar nie. [Tell me, kaffir, this isn't the right leaf, is it?]

BLACK ACTOR: Nee, my Baas. [No, my boss.]

KOTZE: You heard what the kaffir said, Kammel. It's the wrong leaf. Voetsek, kaffer! [Bugger off, kaffir.]

The BLACK ACTOR *gives* KOTZE *the fascist salute. As he turns* KOTZE *kicks him in the backside.*

BLACK ACTOR [*smiling*]: Dankie Baas. Umsunu kanyoko! [Thank you, boss. Your mother's cunt!]

KOTZE *tries to kick him again, but the* BLACK ACTOR *is too nimble and makes off, cheerfully insulting* KOTZE *in Zulu.*

KOTZE: Don't just stand there with your thumb in your bum and your mind in neutral, Kammel. Fetch me the other leaf.

They stare hard at each other.

Don't think it, Kammel. Just go fetch me that leaf.

CAMPBELL *starts running off.*

Kammel, kom hier!

CAMPBELL *returns and halts in front of* KOTZE.

[*quietly*] Fall in, Kammel.

CAMPBELL *joins the platoon.*

Bors uit, pens in, poephol opgeknoop! [Chest out, guts in, arsehole buttoned up!] You cunts think the army's a big fucking joke and you laugh on the other side of your face. I tell you there's a war going on and you think it's not your problem. But if they send you lot to the border you be a sitting duck for that terrorists. They may be stupid kaffirs but they been trained in Russia. Any questions? Right, park your arses in the dirt.

They sit at KOTZE's feet in such a way that he can play this directly to the audience.

I find cunts like Mowbray and Levitt shaming the white race on guard duty. As of from now on I'm putting my foot down with a firm hand. Why do you think we stand guard? Anyone?

MARAIS *raises his hand.*

Badenhorst?

BADENHORST: To be vigilant and alert at all times and to defend ...

KOTZE: Don't talk shit to a white man. Do you want your sister to marry a Russian?

BADENHORST: No, Bombardier.

KOTZE: Then read your newspapers! That terrorists is going to Russia for training and then coming back here to stir shit. There is two kinds of terrorists. Namely, dead terrorists and live terrorists. The second two of these kinds is the problem. They just want to kill and destroy. And the rest of the world is two-face. It just turn its back on South Africa. So we on our own. And remember, if that enemy get past you, he's going to rape your mother and your sister and burn your house. Any questions?

CAMPBELL: Do you really believe that, Bombardier?

KOTZE: Dear Jesus, why do you send me cunts like this? Kammel, kom hier!

CAMPBELL *gets up and goes to* KOTZE.

You just volunteered to show us how to stand guard. That's your beat. Get your arse in gear.

CAMPBELL *starts walking.* KOTZE *starts laughing.*

Ag, nee wat. [Oh, man.] Kammel, you the biggest bloody joke since one-man-one-vote. What's he forgotten, Levitt?

LEVITT: To fix his bayonet, Bombardier.

KOTZE: Pull up your sock, Kammel. Fix that bayonet and hold that rifle like a man. It's your wife.

CAMPBELL *follows the instructions, but his manner remains defiant.*

You don't believe in it, Kammel. All South Africa place its trust in you and you going to let the side down. Badenhorst, go fetch me some grass and mud.

BADENHORST *runs off.*

Now, for the love of Mike, Kammel, just look and learn.

KOTZE *takes Campbell's rifle and demonstrates.*

Be alert, because your enemy is. Hold your rifle at the ready. Balance your weight good, toes and heels. Go through your knees a bit, ready for everything. [*He demonstrates.*] Always keep your back covered. Never stand still. Don't make yourself a easy target.

BADENHORST *returns with a handful of mud, branches and tufts of grass. As he approaches,* KOTZE *spins around and points the rifle at him.*

Halt! Name, rank and number? Halt!

KOTZE *cocks the rifle.*

BADENHORST: Badenhorst, gunner, 65403743.

KOTZE: If that had been for real, half of you would be hanging up a tree. Kammel, vat jou geweer. [Take your rifle.]

He throws the rifle back to CAMPBELL.

Give me this mud. Stuff that branches under his staaldak [steel helmet].

While BADENHORST *does this,* KOTZE *blackens* CAMPBELL's *hands and face with mud.*

Now you don't look like a girl guide try and act like a soldier.

CAMPBELL *makes little attempt to follow these instructions.*

Septic! On your feet, you lot. Kammel wants you to run round the shithouse. Is julle al terug? [Are you back yet?]

The others mutter curses as they run off. KOTZE *manhandles* CAMPBELL *during the following speech.*

You got to hate, Kammel. No other way to survive. Let's see some hate, man. Go on you cunt, eat your liver. Hate, you bangbroek [coward], hate! I shit on your grandmother's grave. I fuck your mother in her mouth. I hold down your sister and rape her up the bum. Hate me, you bastard. Hate me! Let me see your hate. Give me your hate, Kammel, and when the time comes I'll know where to point it. Come on. Come! Hate me. Come. Hate me! Come with your hate. Hate me, you cunt!!

The others enter.

Form up, you cunts. Fix bayonets!

They do so. KOTZE *stands downstage near the sack.*

If I get one good bayonet charge you can go to supper. But let one man give me short and I'll drive you till you drop. Right! The Jew first. And I want to hear you scream. This is SWAPO [South West Africa People's Organisation], Levitt. Kill him!

LEVITT *charges, screams, stabs the sack, but loses his balance and falls.*

You'd be a dead man, Levitt. Roer jou gat! [Move your arse!] Marais, this is MPLA [Mozambique People's Liberation Army]. Kill him!

MARAIS *charges, screams and stabs the sack.*

Mowbray, this is PAC [Pan Africanist Congress]. Kill the bastard!

MOWBRAY *does the same.*

Badenhorst, this is ANC [African National Congress]. Kill!

BADENHORST *repeats the actions.*

Right, Kammel. See this cunt here? Don't be scared of it. It won't bite you. So have some fun. Stick it right in. Wriggle it around and give it a good twist. Then tear the fucker wide open and make it bleed. Let's see some of your hate, Kammel. This is me, Kammel.

CAMPBELL *lurches forward, utters a blood-curdling scream, stabs, twists, and disembowels the sack.*

Good, Campbell. Good.

*We gonna shoot those baboon cousins of yours
in Angola.*

Ndino Ndilula (BLACK ACTOR)
and Kaz McFadden (MOWBRAY).

Scene 6

The bungalow. Late evening. MARAIS, *wearing shorts and a rugby jersey, is alone, reading his Bible. After a while* CAMPBELL *enters carrying a weekend bag.*

MARAIS: Hello Doug.

CAMPBELL: What a luck! A straight-through ride from Durban.

MARAIS: You have a good time?

CAMPBELL: You know then.

MARAIS: I never saw the sea.

CAMPBELL: Hey, well, it's something else.

MARAIS: So you back. I thought you might go AWOL.

CAMPBELL: I'm back.

MARAIS: Tell me, why did you run away?

CAMPBELL: Why do you ask?

MARAIS: Sometimes I just don't know.

CAMPBELL: What?

MARAIS: The army.

CAMPBELL: For sure.

MARAIS: Of course, it does make you a man and that, but why this war?

CAMPBELL: Truly.

Pause.

MARAIS: Are you a religious man, Doug?

CAMPBELL: Well, like within myself I suppose I am. I'm an agnostic.

MARAIS: Practising?

CAMPBELL: Not really.

MARAIS: I believe in the Bible and I been thinking. Here Jesus says: 'Maar ek sê vir julle: julle moet julle vyande liefhê; seën die wat julle vervloek; doen goed aan die wat julle haat en bid vir die wat julle beledig en julle vervolg; sodat julle kinders kan word van julle Vader wat in die hemele is.' ['But I say unto you; love your enemies; bless them that curse you; do good to them that hate you, and pray for them which despitefully use you, and persecute you; that ye may be the children of your Father which is in heaven.'] How can you love your enemy and then kill him?

CAMPBELL: Right.

MARAIS: It doesn't fit.

CAMPBELL: For sure.

MARAIS: Why is everybody against South Africa?

CAMPBELL: Hey man, are you serious?

MARAIS [*sharply*]: Don't laugh at me, Doug.

CAMPBELL: Hey well, I tune you the way I view it: if there was no apartheid, there'd be no war.

MARAIS: In my own life I've never been unkind to the black man.

CAMPBELL: Not you, Paul. Like it's the whole thing.

MARAIS: But there's less apartheid now and there's more war.

CAMPBELL: That's not it.

MARAIS: South Africa is changing. One day the black man will be as equal as the white man.

CAMPBELL: Hey, I've heard that somewhere before.

MARAIS: I'm against apartheid.

CAMPBELL: But you don't mind going up to the border?

MARAIS: You have to defend your country.

CAMPBELL: Is that what you think?

MARAIS: Don't you love South Africa?

CAMPBELL: I don't hate Angola.

MARAIS: That's where the terrorists come from.

44

CAMPBELL: Hey, Paul, think man. What are we doing in Namibia and Angola? We're fighting a colonial war.

MARAIS: But the SWAPO is fighting us.

CAMPBELL: Didn't you say you have to defend your country? Maybe they think like you.

MARAIS: I just don't know.

CAMPBELL: I scheme it's simple.

MARAIS: That's easy for you to say.

CAMPBELL: Hey, where are you coming from?

MARAIS: That's what you told Kotze with your first inspection.

CAMPBELL: What?

MARAIS: That you don't care.

CAMPBELL: What do you know about that? You just do everything you're told and then you come and ask me stupid questions. Like maybe I care about something else than killing people.

MARAIS: I'm not accusing you.

CAMPBELL: Then what's your scene?

MARAIS: I was just asking.

CAMPBELL: Right on! Why don't you Boere ever think? I've got my beliefs, ek sê. And I've been made to suffer for that. First by the MPs [military police] who caught me. They were raw bastards, but it was nothing compared to Pretoria. I gave it to them straight. Like I told them what I schemed on. I said I was totally opposed to the whole concept of Angola, so they sent me to One Mil Hospital. And me, I thought I was crafty. I had a rap with this psychiatrist and I tuned him this and that and blocked for Africa. Like if you had to pretend you were fucked in the head to be exempted from killing people, I could get into that.

Pause.

Hey, but it wasn't like that. The army schemed we were bent and we'd been sent there to be straightened out. They'd been feeding me on medication, these full-on downers, like to break my resistance. One day I was lying spaced out on my bed and this oke came in. He walked in and he was crying. So I said to him, hey what's the matter? Ek sê Paul, he had three doses of shock treatment for refusing to go to Angola and he was expecting his fourth.

MARAIS: Where did they shock him?

CAMPBELL: In the brain.

MARAIS: Did he tell you?

CAMPBELL: I couldn't really kind of communicate with him. He just put his hands to his head and said three times.

MARAIS: Did they do that to you?

CAMPBELL: Naught. When I sussed what was going on, hey like I just tuned what they wanted to hear. No one can handle those shocks.

MARAIS: Why would people do that?

CAMPBELL *shrugs*.

A pause.

Hey, Paul, I'm sorry about what I said.

MARAIS: Wasn't it true?

CAMPBELL: About the Boere.

MARAIS: No, that's all right.

CAMPBELL: For sure.

MARAIS: I like you, Doug. I didn't meet so many English people before.

CAMPBELL: Hey then.

MARAIS: I just thought I'd say so.

BADENHORST and **MOWBRAY** *[enter, singing to the tune of* She'll Be Coming Round The Mountain]:
She'll be all wet and sticky when she comes … etc.

BADENHORST [*holding his middle finger under* Marais*'s nose*]: Smell the good times!

CAMPBELL: Howzit?

MOWBRAY: Grand like a piano.

BADENHORST: She just sucked in my balls and spat out the pips.

MOWBRAY: We only had a good time.

MARAIS: Doug here went to Durban and back.

CAMPBELL: From door to door with this cat in a Porsche.

BADENHORST: Did I ever tell you about the time I got a lift with this goose in a E-type? There was about ten ous standing at the bypass there and she just pulled up by me and said hop in. And she was a sharp bokkie [pretty girl], I'm telling you; fucking blonde hair with this short skirt and shit-hot legs. And you know how you sit really low in a E-type and the pedals are far away? So when she pushes in the clutch hey, and she has to stretch far forward, this bloody skirt slides up and man ...

ALL: She's got no fucking panties on!

They all laugh at BADENHORST.

BADENHORST: I'm never going to tell you ous nothing from now on.

CAMPBELL: Hey, is that a promise?

BADENHORST: Just los me out. [Just leave me alone.] You ous know fuck all about women.

LEVITT *enters carrying parcels.*

LEVITT: Hi there ous.

CAMPBELL: Is it all fixed up with Sharon?

LEVITT: Yes and no. Sometimes I just don't understand women.

MARAIS: Then you better ask old Badenhorst. He's the expert around here.

BADENHORST: Go fuck your hand.

LEVITT: There you are, Paul.

BADENHORST: What's he getting?

MARAIS: But it's mooi [nice], hey.

CAMPBELL: Hey then, the Star of David.

MARAIS: It's a sort of Jewish St Christopher.

BADENHORST: What the Jews will think of next.

MARAIS: No man, it brings good luck.

MOWBRAY: It didn't bring the Yids much luck.

BADENHORST: Is he the only one who gets something?

LEVITT: For you, Hennie.

LEVITT *gives* BADENHORST *a copy of* Playboy.

BADENHORST: Yislaaik hey Davy, thanks a span.

MOWBRAY: Don't get bladdy caught with that, hey.

BADENHORST: Where you come by this, Davy?

LEVITT: I got my connections.

BADENHORST: Paul, look here man. Kom kyk vir hierdie slymsloot. [Come and look at this cunt.]

MARAIS: Suck eggs.

LEVITT: And here's a cake for all of us to share. The old lady forced me to take it with.

CAMPBELL: Hey, lekker [nice]!

LEVITT *places a wonderful cake on a trunk which they slide into the walkway to serve as a table.*

LEVITT: Give us your knife there, Paul. You too, Trevor.

MOWBRAY: No well thanks, ja okay.

MARAIS: You cut, Davy.

BADENHORST: Man, I've got a family-size Fanta. Let's make it an occasion.

CAMPBELL: Truly, like a min-dae feast. [Few days left.]

BADENHORST: Baie dae, min hare [Many days, little hair.]

They talk with their mouths full.

MARAIS: Your Ma bakes nicely.

CAMPBELL: For sure.

BADENHORST: It's bloody lekker, man.

LEVITT: She's a Jewish Mama.

BADENHORST: Well, you can say what you like about the Jews, but they know how to bake cakes.

During the above CAMPBELL *has started tapping on the trunk with his fingers. The rhythm is that of a train's wheels on the track. They all join in the game.*

CAMPBELL: Hey listen!

MARAIS: What's that?

CAMPBELL: Can you hear it?

MARAIS: Luister na die spore. [Listen to the railway tracks.]

They put their ears to the trunk.

BADENHORST: It's coming this way.

LEVITT: What is it?

CAMPBELL: Louis, the min-dae train!

LEVITT: Taking us home!

MOWBRAY: Send it!

They all laugh and start pounding out the rhythm. KOTZE *has been standing in the doorway. He is in civilian clothing and wears a ten-gallon hat. He has been drinking and has a beer in his hand.* MARAIS *sees him.*

MARAIS: Aandag!

The men spring to attention around the cake.

KOTZE: I hope I'm not disturbing. This all looks very cosy. But don't let me disturb you. Carry on.

He advances into the room.

Anyone got a smoke to spare?

A few packets of cigarettes appear. He makes for CAMPBELL.

Thank you, Campbell. Offer them round. Let's have a smoke break.

CAMPBELL *holds up a match to* KOTZE's *cigarette. He takes* CAMPBELL *by the wrist.*

You quite hardegat [hard-arsed], Campbell. But you shaping up nicely. You starting to understand team spirit.

CAMPBELL *pulls his hand away.* KOTZE *sits down on Marais's bed. He takes a drag, puts the cigarette in his ear and blows smoke out through his nose. Not much of a laugh. A silence.*

I been in the fucking army fifteen fucking years. The best fucking years of my fucking life. Gone. Finish and klaar. Gone. Gone.

Pause.

Gone. What you got to say about that?

Long pause.

BADENHORST: Ja, nee, that's life hey.
KOTZE: You know something about life, Badenhorst?
BADENHORST: Ag, you know.
KOTZE: We all listening.
BADENHORST: Just trying to look on the sunny side.

Pause.

And learning to take the rough with the smooth.

KOTZE: Where you get that from? Life's as rough as a pig's back. I joined up after I got my JC [junior certificate – an exam which was written in Grade 8]. I done every bloody course the army's got to offer. I did the instructor's course, machine-gun course, anti-aircraft course, anti-tank course, signals course, maintenance course, field-gunnery course, mortar-bomb course ...

CAMPBELL: Intercourse?

KOTZE [*deadpan*]: The lot. But I didn't got a matric. And I was even in Angola when the government said we wasn't there. I could write a book about Angola. Fifteen years and I still only got two stripes. So just don't talk to me about life. What would you do in my place?

Pause.

Tell me.

MOWBRAY: Why do you stay in the army then, Bombardier?

KOTZE: If you thought like a soldier you wouldn't ask me that.

Pause.

You want to know why?

MOWBRAY: Ja, Bombardier.

KOTZE: Because I hate civilians.

KOTZE *gets up and starts prowling around.*

Who of you's got a woman?

BADENHORST: I'm a married man, Bombardier.

KOTZE: And how does that feel?

BADENHORST: Ja, well, you know.

KOTZE: Next time see if it smells different. Maybe you stirring the cold porridge.

He stops in front of the cake.

51

What's this cake?

LEVITT: You want a piece, Bombardier?

KOTZE: Your girl make this, Levitt?

He stamps on the cake.

What you bringing this woman rubbish in here? This is a army camp. Don't dirty this bungalow up with bitch cakes.

Pause.

You been on pass, but I got a small little secret for you. You all on standby. You know what that means? You going to the border.

Pause.

That's the good news. The bad news is I signed on for another fifteen years. I'll be going with. So if that terrorists don't get you, I will. And you better remember one thing. Don't ever start talking to me about women again.

KOTZE *turns at the doorway.*

You back in the army now.

KOTZE *leaves.*

The men get up quietly, gather up their kit, put on their helmets. There's a change in the lighting state, suggesting time has passed.

CAMPBELL *and* LEVITT *move down stage.*

LEVITT: Sharon said she'd wait for me.

CAMPBELL: Well, there you go.

LEVITT: She won't.

CAMPBELL: Hey well.

LEVITT: I wish I had a broken leg, a dislocated hip, a hunchback, one eye ...

CAMPBELL: Hey, man!

LEVITT: No, anything to get out of it.

CAMPBELL: Whew, heavy.

MOWBRAY [*joins them, drinking a Coke*]: You talking about me?

LEVITT: Don't flatter yourself.

MOWBRAY: I can't offer because it's full of backwash.

CAMPBELL: Safe.

MOWBRAY: If they hadn't kicked me out of the Bats I'd be a border veteran by now.

LEVITT: Or in a plastic bag.

MOWBRAY: Fuck, you ous, you know.

BADENHORST *and* MARAIS *move downstage, carrying a steel trunk between them.*

MARAIS: Where's the Bedford?

BADENHORST: Selle ou storie [same old story], hurry up and wait.

They sit in silence. The BLACK ACTOR *crosses the stage.*

MOWBRAY: Hey Sambo, kom hier! [come here!]

BLACK ACTOR: Did the baas want something?

MOWBRAY: What you fucken doing here, hey?

BLACK ACTOR: The baas, he is say I must fetch that things for to put in the Bedford.

MOWBRAY: Don't talk shit to a white man.

BLACK ACTOR: It's as true as God. I'm telling you.

BADENHORST: Hey, what's your name? You John?

BLACK ACTOR: No Baas, my name it's Sam.

MOWBRAY: What baas sent you?

BLACK ACTOR: I don't know what is he called. The stupid one.

MOWBRAY: Jy raak wit. [You're getting white.]

CAMPBELL: Hey friend, don't I know you?

BLACK ACTOR: No Baas. You don't know me, Baas.

CAMPBELL: Didn't you bring the drinks?

BLACK ACTOR: Aikona! [No!] Never, my Baas. I'm not do that.

CAMPBELL: Hey then, but I know you, ek sê.

BLACK ACTOR: No, Baas. Maybe that man, he was my cousin.

MOWBRAY: Hey Sambo! You know what we gonna do? We gonna shoot those baboon cousins of yours in Angola.

BLACK ACTOR: Baas?

MOWBRAY: You better be a good boy or you get the same. See?

CAMPBELL: Cut it out, Trevor.

MOWBRAY: Before he fucks off I want to see a kaffir dance.

BADENHORST: Ag Trev, the ou's got work to do.

MOWBRAY *points his rifle at the* BLACK ACTOR.

MOWBRAY: Let's see you do a war dance.

MARAIS: Put down that rifle.

MOWBRAY: Fuck you. It's a free country.

LEVITT: What's the ou done to you?

MOWBRAY: I want to see what you people do before you fight.

BADENHORST: Listen Sam, don't worry over him, see. I give you this packet of smokes if you dance.

MOWBRAY: That's a offer you can't refuse.

BLACK ACTOR: I'm not smoke, Baas.

MOWBRAY: He's a clever kaffir.

BADENHORST: Here's fifty cents then.

He throws the coin at the Black Actor*'s feet.*

Do a gumboot dance.

MOWBRAY: Here's some more. Give the kaffir some start, you buggers. Don't be so bladdy Jewish.

The BLACK ACTOR *does a gumboot dance. The others also throw coins at his feet. The dance becomes increasingly defiant and explosive.*

Blackout.

The BLACK ACTOR *continues dancing.*

The soldiers have gone. He stops dancing. He leaves the stage.

She's an imposter.

André Lötter (BADENHORST)

Scene 7

An improvised canteen, somewhere on the border. Sounds of the African night provided throughout this scene by a buzz-track. The men wear floppy bush hats and have their rifles with them at all times. The disco version of The Lion Sleeps Tonight *(by Tight Fit) is heard over the loudspeakers. The music switches to a portable radio on the stage as the lights snap on to reveal BADENHORST dancing on a table. His trousers are in a pool around his* ankles *and his genitals are tucked between his legs to create the illusion of a vagina.*

CAMPBELL and **MOWBRAY** [*shouting*]: Take it off! Take it off! Take it off! Take it off!

BADENHORST *removes his bush hat, performs a lewd ritual with it and throws it to* MARAIS.

Show us some more! Show us some more!

BADENHORST *twists around, bends over and exposes his backside and genitals.*

CAMPBELL: Hey then, she's an impostor.
MOWBRAY: Don't strangle your dangle.

BADENHORST *takes his rifle in one hand and his genitals in the other.*

BADENHORST [*chanting*]: This is my rifle. This is my gun. This is for shooting. This is for fun!

LEVITT *enters during the above. He turns the radio off.*

LEVITT: The batteries.

An awkward silence. BADENHORST *pulls up his trousers.*

MARAIS: Dave, come pull up a chair, man.

BADENHORST: Back to the States tomorrow, Davy.

CAMPBELL: Don't count on it.

LEVITT *sits. He is withdrawn and edgy.*

BADENHORST: Okay, beach bum, pay up.

CAMPBELL: I had my fingers crossed.

BADENHORST: Twenty-five rand.

CAMPBELL: You gyppoed [cheated].

BADENHORST: Twenty-five rand!

CAMPBELL: I said to the end of the song.

BADENHORST [*indicating* LEVITT]: Ja, but he ... No, listen, my man.

CAMPBELL: You blew it.

BADENHORST: You sailing for a nailing.

CAMPBELL: Like listen. If you do it again, but properly, you'll get your bread.

BADENHORST: I know you, Campbell. You full of shit. One day you'll come short.

CAMPBELL: Give us a kiss.

BADENHORST: Watch it!

MARAIS: Never mind, Hennie. I thought you was good in the dancing.

BADENHORST: Go jump at a lake.

Silence, boredom and restlessness.

Five months without a poke.

LEVITT: What?

BADENHORST: Must be my record, man.

MARAIS: Moenie worry nie. Alles sal regkom. [Don't worry. Everything will come right.]

BADENHORST: Suid-Wes? Tuis Bes! [South-West? Home Best!]

CAMPBELL: I don't scheme we're splitting tomorrow.

MOWBRAY: Maybe we get a chance to waste some kaffirs first.

MARAIS: Tomorrow we go home.

CAMPBELL: Roll on tomorrow.

MOWBRAY: If you don't want your beer, Levitt, I'll buy it off you.

LEVITT: What?

A silence. Levitt's mood is making them uncomfortable.

BADENHORST: You ous heard of Russian roulette, hey? You know what's South African roulette? You find a kaffir girl and take it into a public phone box. You pull down her panties, stick in your cock, phone the police and see who comes first.

MOWBRAY: You got kaffir girls on the brain.

BADENHORST: It's also pink inside.

Pause.

MOWBRAY: Hey Levitt, can I buy that beer off you?

LEVITT: No, I want it.

MOWBRAY: All of a sudden he wants it. Typical Jewboy!

MARAIS: Leave him. It's his beer.

A strained silence.

BADENHORST: Hey, you know what I'll do when I get home? First thing, I'll get the wife to run me a bath. Nice and full of hot water. I'll get in there with a six-pack of Carling Black Labels [beers]. And while she's in the kitchen making my favourite food I'll sommer [just] just lay there farting and biting the bubbles. Then on comes the graze. I'll sit down to roast mutton, potatoes, rice, carrots, peas and beans, sweet potatoes, pumpkin and all that covered with a lekker, dik [thick] gravy. And when I've finished eating, the wife will slip off to the bedroom. A soft bed, crispy, white sheets and her just laying there in this thin nightie. Five months I've been waiting for this! Hell of a slowly she pulls off the nightie. She's laying there against the pillows. She opens her knees slightly and you hear this soft sucking sound as the lips pull apart.

He looks at the others, who have all been listening intently.

You find this interesting? You want to hear more? Sorry, but it's my wife we're talking about.

CAMPBELL: It's enough to put anyone off sex.

BADENHORST: I'll slap you down, my man.

MOWBRAY: She sounds like a good fuck.

BADENHORST [*sharply*]: Watch it!

LEVITT: I wonder what it's like to die.

A gentle shock wave.

They say you never hear the one that kills you.

MARAIS: Who can ever tell us that?

LEVITT: It must burn.

BADENHORST: Change the subject.

LEVITT: I won't cross that river again.

MARAIS: That's so. Tomorrow we go back the other side of the line.

LEVITT: I don't care what they do, I won't cross that border again.

CAMPBELL: Cool it, Dave. If you're feeling stretched, go to the Sick Bay and ask for something.

LEVITT: You think I can't take it?

CAMPBELL: Hey, no.

MARAIS: Think of it, Dave. Home sweet home.

LEVITT: I'm not going into Angola again.

MOWBRAY [*chicken imitation*]: Pukaak, puk, puk, puk!

BADENHORST: Davy, look on the sunny side, man. Our rear echelon has never taken casualties.

LEVITT: If my petrol truck took a hit, it would burn.

CAMPBELL: Hey Dave, like we're all in the same boat.

LEVITT: Are we?

CAMPBELL: For sure.

LEVITT: And what do you feel about it then?

CAMPBELL: Hey, well.

LEVITT: No, I'm asking you straight. You were the big rebel. You've got the black friends. You didn't believe in this war. Have you changed your mind?

CAMPBELL: Hey Dave, don't lay this heavy trip on me.

LEVITT: I just thought you had principles.

CAMPBELL: Within myself I've got principles, ek sê. But like here we've just got to survive.

LEVITT: And your principles?

CAMPBELL: Whew, heavy.

BADENHORST: That's just only because he's got the wrong principle. My principle is still the same. Those Russians come here to make trouble with the black. They want to take over South Africa. Then I say: over my dead body.

CAMPBELL: Go and fuck yourself, Badenhorst.

LEVITT: Is this something you're prepared to die for, Doug?

CAMPBELL: No way.

LEVITT: Then how come you're here?

CAMPBELL: Hey then, what are the options?

LEVITT: You know them.

CAMPBELL: Like Dave, I tune you straight. We've like passed the stage of scheming why we're here. We are, ek sê. That's our reality. It's like a choice between life and death. And I'm scheming on getting out of here alive.

MARAIS [*shouting*]: Relax man, you ous!

Silence.

> We done our bit. Think of the future. When we stand up tomorrow, we go south. In Grootfontein there's a C-130 standing on the runway. And you know man, it's waiting to take us home.

BADENHORST [*breaking the mood with a chuckle*]: That reminds me. Davy, did you hear the one about this ou who went to a prossie?

The others groan. BADENHORST *steams ahead.*

> Anyway, he's been sitting in this bar all night getting lekker cut [drunk]. So he phones up this prossie and says: No man, I'm here in this bar and I'm feeling randy as a dog, so I'm coming round for a fuck just now. Well, she can't say no, but she hears on the phone he's as pissed as a fart, so she plans to play a trick on him. She's got one of these life-size rubber dolls what you blow up, so she just stuffs it in the bed. Now when this ou comes there, and he's really cut hey, she says: Listen, I'm sorry but it's my time of the month, I got the drips badly, so if you don't mind, why don't you just poke my sister? She's a really very sexy bokkie with a sharp personality and she's just laying in the bed waiting for you. Well, meat is meat and a man must eat, so he says: Dop, doos en doringdraad [drink, pussy and barbed wire] and he's into that bedroom like a pig into shit. Two minutes later he comes running kaalgat [naked] out the room. What's the matter? asks the prossie. No man, says the ou, but you got a funny sister. I climbed on top of her, bit her on the tit, then she farted and flew out the window.

All, except LEVITT, laugh at the joke.

MOWBRAY: Don't you find it funny, Levitt?

LEVITT: What?

MOWBRAY: He's in a dwaal [daze].

MARAIS: Los him, Trevor.

The restless boredom re-establishes itself. The silence is oppressive. MOWBRAY *drains a can of beer, holds it like a hand grenade, performs an elaborate mime of withdrawing the pin and hurls it against the wall.*

MOWBRAY: Aitsaa!

LEVITT *dives to the floor.*

BADENHORST: Fuck off, you!

MOWBRAY: He's gone to ground.

MARAIS: Shut up, you bloody fool.

CAMPBELL: Hey like Dave, it was nothing.

LEVITT *is sobbing hysterically.*

BADENHORST: Give the man air.

MOWBRAY: It's just a bladdy act, man.

BADENHORST [*to* MOWBRAY]: Listen here, you go see if you can find Kotze by the Duty Officer there. I'll go to the NCO mess. And you ous, for fuck's sake, just stay with him hey.

BADENHORST *and* MOWBRAY *leave.*

MARAIS: Put your head in your knees and breathe deep.

LEVITT: I don't give a fuck. I don't give a fuck. I don't give a fuck.

CAMPBELL: Take it easy, Dave.

LEVITT: I don't give a fuck. I'm going to tell them.

CAMPBELL: Naught, Dave. Tune them nothing.

LEVITT: I won't die for those bastards.

CAMPBELL: Dave, don't say nothing about refusing.

LEVITT: I'll tell him the truth.

CAMPBELL: Hey, pal, you out of your mind, man.

LEVITT: You think I'm mad? You're fucking mad. This whole fucking war's fucking mad.

CAMPBELL: Hey, like I know, Dave.

LEVITT: Then why don't you say so?

CAMPBELL: Hey Dave, think man! Kotze doesn't scheme like that. He'll drop you in the shit.

LEVITT: It's the truth.

CAMPBELL: Hey, the truth won't help you. If you tell them that they'll shock your brain.

LEVITT: They can do what they like.

CAMPBELL: Dave, like I've seen what they do to ous.

LEVITT: I'll do nothing for them.

CAMPBELL: Don't give them a reason.

LEVITT: Nothing!

CAMPBELL: Why won't you listen to me?

LEVITT: What have you got to say for yourself?

Pause.

You're taken. The big rebel! They've got you just where they want you.

CAMPBELL: Don't give me that shit.

MOWBRAY *enters.*

LEVITT: Where's Kotze? Where's the little Hitler? He can stick his war up his arse. I'm finished with it. So far and no further. What are we doing here? This isn't even our country.

Suddenly he starts singing, loudly, almost to the point of shouting. The tune is Oh My Darlin' Clementine.

Fuck the army, fuck the army
Fuck the army through and through

I would rather be a civvy

Than an army cunt like you

MARAIS: Dave, listen, stay here.

LEVITT: Leave me alone!

MARAIS *slaps* Levitt'*s face.* LEVITT *makes a dash for the door.*
MARAIS *runs after him, drags him back into the room, and floors*
him with a punch.

MARAIS: Why do you make me do this?

MOWBRAY [*gets down next to* LEVITT *like a boxing referee and*
starts counting]: One ... Two ... Three ...

MARAIS: Shut up!

MOWBRAY: The oke's busy going mad.

MARAIS [*jumping at* MOWBRAY, *knocking him off balance so*
he falls to the ground, and standing over him]: Listen to me,
Mowbray, and you better listen good. You knew what was with
him and still you threw that can. You playing dirty. But that's the
last time. When Kotze comes, you heard nothing and you saw
nothing. Understand what I'm saying?

MOWBRAY: What do you take me for?

MARAIS: One word and I'll find you.

MOWBRAY: I wasn't gonna to say nothing.

BADENHORST *enters.* KOTZE *follows him on. He doesn't wear*
rank on the border.

KOTZE: What seems to be the problem?

He crosses to LEVITT.

You not dying there, are you, Levitt?

MARAIS: He was beside himself, so I was forced to restrain him.

KOTZE: It's not just a gyppo [sham]?

MARAIS: I think it's shell shock.

KOTZE: Well, a qualified doctor will find out quick enough. Come on, my boy. We'll have you fighting fit in no time. Get the man to Sick Bay.

BADENHORST: Paul, give us a hand.

BADENHORST *and* MARAIS *lift* LEVITT.

KOTZE: Wag 'n bietjie. [Wait a bit.] What made him go funny?

CAMPBELL: He threw a can against the wall.

MOWBRAY: I never did it on purpose.

KOTZE [*harshly*]: You a cunt, Mowbray.

MOWBRAY: I never knew.

KOTZE: What are you?

MOWBRAY: Swear to God.

KOTZE: What are you?

MOWBRAY: A cunt.

KOTZE: Well, don't just stand there. Get that man out of here. Move, you dumb cunts.

BADENHORST *and* MARAIS *go off with* LEVITT.

Well, war sorts out the weeds from the men. Mowbray, for fuck's sake, don't sulk. Get some beers, man. It's on me.

KOTZE *picks up playing cards from the table.*

Tell me, Campbell, you think Levitt's really bosbefok [lit. bush mad or form of combat stress]?

CAMPBELL: He's stretched.

MOWBRAY: It's 'cause his chick's going it with a other ou.

KOTZE: Ja nee. In Israel those Jewboys neuk [beat] up the Arab good and proper, but here they a dead loss.

KOTZE *sits and lights a cigarette.*

CAMPBELL: Are we splitting to the States [South Africa] tomorrow, Bombardier?

KOTZE [*impishly*]: That's a military secret, jong [boy]. That's a military secret.

CAMPBELL: Like it's what we heard.

KOTZE: Don't believe all the rumours of war.

KOTZE *smiles, takes a drag, puts the cigarette in his ear and exhales through his nose. A laugh from* MOWBRAY. *With the cigarette still in his ear* KOTZE *starts dealing cards for a poker game.*

You men a bit homesick, hey?

CAMPBELL: We need to slack out a bit.

KOTZE: What you bid?

CAMPBELL: Five.

They put in matches.

KOTZE: And you, Mowbray?

MOWBRAY: Ag, not really. Only this is a shit country, man. Just bush and bladdy kaffirs.

KOTZE: I wasn't asking that.

MOWBRAY: Well, that's just how I feel.

KOTZE: Are you playing?

MOWBRAY: No ja okay fine.

KOTZE: What are the stakes?

CAMPBELL: Life and death?

KOTZE [*an ugly laugh*]: You sure you can meet that challenge, Campbell? No. I'll raise you five.

CAMPBELL: I'll see that and raise you fifty.

KOTZE: Fuck me.

MOWBRAY: He's chaffing.

KOTZE: You bluffing, Campbell?

CAMPBELL: Try me.

MOWBRAY: See him!

KOTZE: I can read you like a book, Campbell.

CAMPBELL: Hey well, I didn't think you'd find it that difficult.

KOTZE: What you trying to say?

CAMPBELL: One rand a match.

MOWBRAY: I fold.

CAMPBELL: Just you and me, Bombardier.

KOTZE: That day will come, Campbell.

Pause.

> Cards isn't life. My business is men. And I tell you something for nothing: I always win.

KOTZE *throws in his hand.*

CAMPBELL: Hey, Bombardier, like you know what's going on here and all that shit. With the war and that.

KOTZE: What's your problem?

CAMPBELL: Like it's something I heard and I was trying to scheme whether it was true.

KOTZE: Campbell, jong, you know I can't divulge military secrets.

CAMPBELL: Hey, for sure. But like this is different. It's about this bombardier in Rundu. They say he gave his men a hard time.

KOTZE: Who's this?

CAMPBELL: Like I forget the name, but they say that while they were out on an Op he was shot down by his own men.

Pause.

> Like I just wondered if that actually happened.

KOTZE [*deliberately*]: We South Africans don't go in for that kind of thing, Campbell.

Silence. CAMPBELL *and* KOTZE *are watching each other.*

MOWBRAY: What's going on?

A series of deafening bangs. CAMPBELL *and* MOWBRAY *dive to the floor. They grab their rifles and scramble to the dug-out section.* KOTZE *stands petrified in the middle of the floor. They all speak in stage whispers.*

CAMPBELL: Take cover, you cunt!

KOTZE: The bastards are shooting at us.

CAMPBELL: Take cover.

CAMPBELL *lunges forward and pulls* KOTZE *to the floor. There is another series of bangs.*

KOTZE: Those are Stalin Organs.

CAMPBELL: Shut up!

KOTZE: Ja, careless talk costs lives. That was a narrow shave.

CAMPBELL: Christ.

KOTZE: Thanks, hey Campbell, thanks. I won't forget you.

There is another series of bangs, then the muffled pounding of artillery fire takes over and continues to the end of the scene.

Vasbyt, manne! [Hang in there, men!]

MOWBRAY: Are those our boys?

KOTZE: Everything's under control now. [*He gets up and dusts himself off.*] Better strip down and oil those rifles. Come, come. Snap out of it, men. You be needing them just now.

BADENHORST [*bursting in*]: O God. O God.

KOTZE: What's the trouble?

BADENHORST: I shat myself.

KOTZE: What?

BADENHORST: We took some hits, but I didn't see what. I was coming across the vehicle park. I ran to a trench. Then I, man I bloody shat myself.

MARAIS *enters. He is covered in grime and mud.*

KOTZE: You all right, Marais?

MARAIS: They hit the bungalow. I don't know, I think ten are killed.

Pause.

I'm dreaming.

Pause.

Hands! Hands!

He hits himself in the face.

Hands! Hands!

He continues hitting himself in the face. KOTZE *grabs him by the wrists.*

KOTZE: Pull yourself together.

MARAIS [*matter of fact*]: Dave is dead.

KOTZE: Who?

MARAIS: The blast hit him in the back. He was already running. He was all burnt.

KOTZE: Listen here. You a first-class bunch of men. I been meaning to tell you that. Just now we crossing the border and I could say I'm proud to have you boys riding with. As for, um, Dave ... Well, that's life. Now it's over to us. We must show he didn't die for nothing.

Pause.

I can't read minds, but to look at you I say we now all want the same thing: a communist to kill.

Blackout. The sound of hectic small-arms fire, followed by the sound of a motor, which defines itself as an excavator. As the next scene begins, this sound is softer but remains present until the end of the play.

Come on, die for your country..

Dylan Horley (CAMPBELL) and Ndino Ndilula (BLACK ACTOR).

Scene 8

Lights up on the shelled-out remains of a Portuguese trading store in the south of Angola. Rubble on the floor. MOWBRAY *is on a looting spree. He finds a framed photograph on the floor. He sits on a wooden crate and cleans the frame with his handkerchief. After a moment* CAMPBELL *and* MARAIS *enter. All the men are soiled and wear full battle kit.*

MARAIS: Is that the last box?
MOWBRAY: Check this, man. A fucken Portugoose.

They look at the photograph.

> His wife's a fucken pig. I wouldn't rape her if you tied her down for me.

MARAIS: Where are they now?
MOWBRAY: Pushing up daisies.

MOWBRAY *breaks the glass that covers the photograph and holds up the frame.*

> This is silver this. Man, this place is full of stuff the kaffirs didn't know about.

MOWBRAY *puts the frame inside his shirt.*

> See if you can find any more stuff here. I'm going on a private search-and-destroy mission. Just don't hang around too bladdy long, hey. We got to stand to at last light and the bommie says before we pull out we putting the base to the torch.

MOWBRAY *picks up his rifle and leaves.* CAMPBELL *stumbles to a corner and vomits.* MARAIS *watches him, then lifts a corner of the crate.*

MARAIS: It's heavy.

CAMPBELL *takes a sip from his water bottle, rinses his mouth, spits and drinks.*

White people lived here.

Pause.

What happened to them?

CAMPBELL: What happened to us?

MARAIS: They gone.

CAMPBELL: You know, when Dave got killed ...

MARAIS: What?

CAMPBELL: When Dave got killed the first thing I thought was: thank God it wasn't me.

MARAIS: It's a sin.

CAMPBELL: Naught. It was a blind thing to think.

MARAIS: It's a sin.

CAMPBELL: What?

MARAIS: There was children there.

CAMPBELL: Hey, when this is over.

MARAIS: Why children?

CAMPBELL: Never again.

MARAIS: I saw it, man.

CAMPBELL: When we get home.

MARAIS: What have we done?

CAMPBELL: I'm leaving the country.

MARAIS: We'll be punished.

CAMPBELL: What are you talking about?

MARAIS: It's a crime.

CAMPBELL: Hey, man.

MARAIS: You can't just do that.

CAMPBELL: What?

MARAIS: Children.

CAMPBELL: We did nothing.

MARAIS: Did you look out your eyes.

CAMPBELL: Hey, you and me, we weren't even there.

MARAIS: Suffer little children.

CAMPBELL: Hey Paul, think man. We pulling out tonight. After this Op they'll send us home. This whole trip will be over, man. Take.

CAMPBELL *hands* MARAIS *his water bottle.* MARAIS *holds it, but doesn't drink.*

MARAIS: Could you kill a defenceless ...

CAMPBELL: For Christ's sake!

MARAIS *notices something on his trouser leg.*

MARAIS: Sis, it's blood.

CAMPBELL: It's just dirt.

MARAIS: No man, it's blood.

MARAIS *starts rubbing the spot.*

CAMPBELL: This is unreal.

MARAIS: It is blood. [*He wets his hat with water from the bottle and starts rubbing the spot.*] It just spreads.

CAMPBELL [*picking up a corner of the crate*]: Come on.

MARAIS: It won't come out.

CAMPBELL: Let's go.

MARAIS: It smells, dammit.

MARAIS *pours the water over his leg.*

CAMPBELL: Hey man, that's water!

CAMPBELL *grabs the water bottle.* MARAIS *won't let go and a tug-o-war ensues. Water splashes all over.*

MARAIS: It's on my skin.

CAMPBELL: Let go!

MARAIS: I'm dirty.

CAMPBELL: Okay Paul, just cool it, hey.

MARAIS: I got blood on me.

CAMPBELL [*wrenching the bottle away from* MARAIS]: This is water, you arsehole.

MARAIS: Onse vader wat in die hemel is, laat u naam geheilig word, laat u konikryk kom, laat u wil geskied, soos in die hemel, so ook op die aarde. Gee ons vandag ons daaglikse brood en vergewe ons ons skulde. En vergewe ons ons skulde. [Our Father who art in heaven, hallowed be thy name. Thy kingdom come. Thy will be done on earth as it is in heaven. Give us this day our daily bread, and forgive us our trespasses.]

CAMPBELL [*tipping the water bottle and discovering it's empty*]: Christ.

MARAIS: Soos ons ook ons skuldenaars vergewe, en lei ons nie in versoeking nie, maar verlos ons van die Bose. Maar verlos ons van die Bose. Maar verlos ons van die Bose. [As we forgive those who trespass against us, and lead us not into temptation, but deliver us from evil. But deliver us from evil. But deliver us from evil.]

CAMPBELL: Stop it!

MARAIS: Maar verlos ons van die Bose.

CAMPBELL *takes* MARAIS *by the shoulders and shakes him.*

Maar verlos ons van die Bose.

The BLACK ACTOR *appears from behind the counter in combat clothing. The front of his shirt is soaked in blood. He points an AK47 rifle at them.*

BLACK ACTOR: Come, come. You like to kill me? You go with me then, hey. Come on, die for your country.

76

Pause.

You scared, little soldiers? Scared of me? I'm the one that got away. I'm not a Cuba. I'm not a Russia. You see what I am?

MARAIS: From the SWAPO?

He laughs and turns on CAMPBELL.

BLACK ACTOR: You! Come here.

Pause.

Come here or I shoot you where you stand.

CAMPBELL *moves to him.*

The word you use for me? What I am.

CAMPBELL: Please ...

BLACK ACTOR [*fiercely*]: Say it!

He puts the barrel of his AK47 to CAMPBELL's *mouth.*

You call me kaffir. Go on. Say it!

CAMPBELL [*almost inaudible*]: Kaffir.

BLACK ACTOR: Look me in my eye, white boy. Give me a good reason why I must not kill you.

The BLACK ACTOR *kicks* CAMPBELL's *feet out from under him, sends him sprawling and shouts.*

If I must die, why must you live?

CAMPBELL: Please, we've done nothing.

BLACK ACTOR: You want to make a deal with me?

CAMPBELL: What?

BLACK ACTOR [*pulling* CAMPBELL *to his knees*]: What must happen if I am your prisoner?

Pause.

What do you do to your prisoners?

CAMPBELL: Please, I ...

BLACK ACTOR: You just shoot them!

The BLACK ACTOR *kicks* CAMPBELL *in the face.*

CAMPBELL: We didn't do anything.

BLACK ACTOR: Can you give me anything, white boy?

Pause.

Maybe I just kill you now.

A long moment in which the only sound is the digging.

What is that noise?

CAMPBELL: We just transport supplies.

BLACK ACTOR: What is that rifle?

CAMPBELL: Truly, we've done nothing.

BLACK ACTOR: What is that uniform?

CAMPBELL: I had no choice.

BLACK ACTOR: They going to come with fire just now. Like always. Maybe we burning together. Or must they come to fetch you? Then you must tell them to go away, or I shoot you first. You can choose.

Pause.

What is that noise?

CAMPBELL: You're wounded.

BLACK ACTOR: Don't worry. It's no matter if I die. You coming with bombs. But you can't kill all African peoples. Tomorrow we still here.

Pause.

What is that noise?

MARAIS: They digging a hole.

BLACK ACTOR: Deep down?

MARAIS: Excuse me?

BLACK ACTOR: Something to hide?

MARAIS: The smell. It's the smell.

BLACK ACTOR: Who are you?

MARAIS: What?

BLACK ACTOR: What is your name?

MARAIS: Paul. My name is Paul.

BLACK ACTOR: It must be deep or the dogs will come and dig it up.

MARAIS: You hurting.

BLACK ACTOR: I don't feel this.

MARAIS: Why?

BLACK ACTOR: Because I know.

MARAIS: What?

BLACK ACTOR: One day you won't be coming here. I know that.

MARAIS: How?

BLACK ACTOR: Because then it will be finish.

MARAIS: When

BLACK ACTOR: One day.

The BLACK ACTOR *tenses. He raises his rifle and points it first at* MARAIS *then at* CAMPBELL. *Suddenly he drops the rifle and clutches his stomach with both hands.* CAMPBELL *leaps forward and retrieves the rifle.* MARAIS *goes to the* BLACK ACTOR.

MARAIS: Give me your hands.

BLACK ACTOR: Why?

CAMPBELL: Paul, we're going.

MARAIS drags the BLACK ACTOR to his feet.

MARAIS: Don't go.

BLACK ACTOR: One day.

MARAIS *staggers across the stage with the* BLACK ACTOR *in his arms; a grotesque* pas de deux.

MARAIS [*shouting*]: Don't go now. What must happen? Tell me! What must I do? What must I do?

The BLACK ACTOR *becomes a dead weight and sags to the floor dragging* MARAIS *with him.* MARAIS *screams and starts sobbing.* MOWBRAY, BADENHORST *and* KOTZE *hurtle into the room and fan out into firing positions. All rifles are pointed at the* BLACK ACTOR.

Before they are quite in position KOTZE *screams.*

KOTZE: Hold your fire! What the fuck's this?
CAMPBELL: It's okay now.
MOWBRAY: It's a fucken terr.
KOTZE: What's with Marais?
CAMPBELL: I don't know.

BADENHORST *crosses to* MARAIS. CAMPBELL *hands the Black Actor's AK47 to* KOTZE.

BADENHORST: Kom boetie [Come, brother], we going.

As BADENHORST *bends over him* MARAIS *lashes out.*

MARAIS: That was children.
BADENHORST: Fuck off.

MARAIS *gets up, utters the bayonet charge scream and rushes at* KOTZE, *knocking him to the floor.*

MARAIS: Children! Children! Children!
KOTZE: Get him off me! Get him off me!

BADENHORST *and* MOWBRAY *grab* MARAIS *and pull him off.*

MARAIS: One day!

KOTZE: Get him out of here!

MARAIS: One day! One day!

BADENHORST *and* MOWBRAY *drag* MARAIS *off.*

KOTZE: Another one completely bosbefok. These bloody children can't take it. So it goes.

Pause.

Finish him off, Campbell.

CAMPBELL: What?

KOTZE: That enemy. You know how to use your bayonet.

CAMPBELL: He's wounded.

KOTZE: Do him a favour then. Put him out of his misery. Give him a bullet.

CAMPBELL: No. I can't.

KOTZE: Yes, you can.

KOTZE *points the Black Actor's AK47 at* CAMPBELL.

It's you or him, Campbell. It always has been.

This tableau is held for a moment, then CAMPBELL *raises the rifle, points it at the* BLACK ACTOR *and fires. As the shot rings out the theatre is plunged into darkness.*

THE END

Afterword

Gary Baines[1]

Somewhere on the Border first appeared as a working script accredited to the Thekwini Theatre Foundation, Amsterdam, in 1983. A version of the script was included in a collection called *South Africa Plays*, edited and introduced by Stephen Gray in 1993. The publication of five landmark plays that had been penned during the dark days of apartheid coincided with the country's first tentative steps towards dismantling a well-entrenched system of white minority rule. Now, some 20 years after the demise of the apartheid regime Anthony Akerman's play is being published as a stand-alone text for the first time.

So why is it an apposite time to republish the script?

This question cannot be answered simply in relation to the publication history of *Somewhere on the Border*, which also has a history of production, performance and reception. While I do not propose to discuss this history in any detail here, the production of *Somewhere on the Border* marks a milestone in South African literary history and cultural memory. This is primarily because of its authenticity and the emotive connection of its historical re-enactment. It conveys a sense of what young white men experienced in the South African Defence Force (SADF).

Conscription, or national service as it was more commonly called, was a rite of passage for a generation of young white males. Between 1968 and 1993 approximately 600 000 boys aged 18 or more donned the nutria brown uniform of the SADF. As far as most of these conscripts were concerned there was no option other than to heed the call-up. Failure to do so meant harsh penalties. The alternatives were to object on conscientious (actually religious) grounds and face a six-year jail sentence, or to flee the country.

Those who went into exile were sometimes accorded the status of political refugees. This implied that asylum seekers effectively disowned their country and its policies.

The obligations of white males who remained in the country did not end with national service. SADF members were assigned to citizen force or commando units and were liable for periodical call-ups for camps. These might have entailed deployment in the 'operational areas' from 1974 against the South West Africa People's Organisation (SWAPO) and thereafter against Angolan forces and their Cuban allies. From 1984 SADF soldiers were equally likely to do tours of duty in the black townships, where they supported the police in crushing resistance to apartheid. Those belonging to the national service generation were part-time or citizen soldiers for much of their adult lives. Most served willingly, some with fervour. Others did so reluctantly and with little enthusiasm.

The SADF gradually extended the period of conscription from nine months to two years as increased demands were made upon a cohort of white males. Many of these men were convinced that it was their patriotic duty to defend their country against the twin threats of communism and African nationalism. They believed that they were protecting the country's borders, although they were deployed primarily in northern Namibia and southern Angola. Here South Africa's (mainly black) surrogate forces bore the brunt of the fighting and sustained the bulk of casualties, while the SADF provided the leadership and an ever-expanding range of sophisticated weaponry. Still, the growing number of deaths of national servicemen on active service, as well as from accidents and suicides, raised the political cost of waging war indefinitely. The military stalemate compelled the politicians to seek a resolution and negotiate a settlement.

Consequently, the Cuban armed forces and the SADF withdrew from Angola in 1988. A ceasefire allowed for the implementation of United Nations Security Council (UNSC) Resolution 435 in Namibia, where SWAPO won the country's internationally-supervised elections. These developments provided impetus for the reformist agenda in South Africa, where the last National Party president, F W de Klerk, reined in the security forces and the liberation movements suspended the armed struggle. The interim power-sharing agreement provided for the integration of the statutory and non-statutory forces into what had become the South African National Defence Force (SANDF). And conscription, which had buttressed the authoritarian apartheid regime for 25 years, was phased out.

With these momentous changes to the political landscape in South Africa, veterans tried to make sense of what they had fought for or the time they had spent in SADF uniform. Many could not understand why they had been asked to sacrifice so much only to surrender power to those whom they had previously regarded as 'the enemy'. Some were convinced that their erstwhile leaders had betrayed them. However, most remained silent: either out of a (misguided?) sense of loyalty to the old regime and fellow soldiers, or for fear of being held accountable by the African National Congress (ANC) government for gross human rights violations.

The veterans' relative silence in the immediate post-apartheid years was partly encouraged by the vision of the Rainbow Nation, with its inclusionary imperative. It was deemed 'politically correct' to emphasise South Africa's commonalities rather than its conflictual past. Yet the climate of reconciliation was undermined by a clique of retired generals who refused to own up to the part played by the SADF and especially by its sinister agencies, such as the Civil Co-Operation Bureau (*sic*), in the systematic abuse of human rights. These same generals also acted as gatekeepers so that professional soldiers and conscripts were deterred from testifying before the Truth and Reconciliation Commission (TRC).

Although the TRC recognised the trauma suffered by conscripts it employed binary categories that classified those who testified before it either as perpetrators or as victims. While ANC government spokespersons have tended to label the SADF the 'apartheid army' and regard its soldiers as tainted by their role in upholding the status quo, many of the veterans have been inclined to embrace victimhood: to regard themselves as having had little choice in respect of the duties they were instructed to perform while they were in the army.

SADF veterans were undoubtedly subjected to indoctrination, which promoted ideological conformity. They might be described as a speech community. To this day their speech is still frequently peppered with expletives, turns of phrase and jargon learned while in uniform. In the army, the arm of the service in which by far the majority of national servicemen rendered their duties, drilling and most commands were delivered and learned only in Afrikaans. Indeed, certain terms such as *ballasbak*, *bosbefok* and *vasbyt* seem to have no English equivalents.

This is not to suggest that the two main language groups necessarily embraced one another. Indeed, differences were accentuated during training, where insults such as *soutpiel* (for English-speakers) and *rocks* (for Afrikaans-speakers) were frequently traded. And they often had little in common in the way of cultural and social background – a point illustrated by the characters in *Somewhere on the Border*. But the fighting unit invariably did develop a camaraderie and loyalty to each other, for the shared experience of the group rather than the common characteristics of individuals created a sense of belonging and identity.

But exactly what stake do veterans have in their militarised identities and memories of their experiences in the SADF? Is it possible to generalise about a group that is by no means homogenous?

SADF veterans have mixed – even contradictory – recollections of their time in uniform: while some look back with sentimentality on this period of their lives, others would rather forget it altogether. Whether these experiences are fondly remembered because of the male bonding of the military environment or regretted as time wasted in defending an unjust system, they left a lasting impression on soldiers. Indeed, it is unrealistic to imagine that veterans have been able to make a seamless transition to civilian life or to attain closure if they suffered the symptoms of combat stress or psychosocial trauma. For the experience of waging war – especially an unjust one in the name of a discredited ideology and an illegitimate regime – has left certain veterans with a residual sense of guilt or shame. Yet others clearly enjoyed the experience and found it positively life-transforming. The issue for veterans, then, is not whether the war was right or wrong but that they were involved; *they were there*. One way or the other, national service proved to be consequential for veterans as individuals, as well for South African society at large.

Whereas certain veterans have been able to adapt to the political transition and commit themselves to making the 'new' South Africa work, others have remained indifferent or opposed to the changes. Some have welcomed South Africa's return to the community of nations and the benefits of globalisation – especially a return to international sporting codes and the lifting of travel restrictions and economic sanctions. Others have left the country. Indeed, white South Africans have become a very mobile group since 1994 and have relocated all over the world. Many veterans have become part of the South African diaspora and have taken their skills elsewhere.

But wherever these veterans find themselves they appear to have a need to connect with those who had similar experiences. This has been made possible by information and communication technologies. Cyberspace has seen the proliferation of internet sites, blogs, discussion (or Google) groups where veterans tell their stories, share their photographs and sound off about all and sundry. The coterie of veterans who associate in this manner sometimes excludes 'outsiders' by invoking the mantra of all soldiers: 'How can you understand? ... You were not there', or its Afrikaans equivalent:

'*Net ons wat in die weermag was weet wat dit is* [Only we who were in the army know what it was like].'

While some ex-soldiers like to close ranks others prefer to share their experiences. The more articulate SADF veterans have discovered their voices in older forms of media such as novels, memoirs and histories of specific units (especially the Special Forces – popularly known as the 'recces'). Apart from literature, veterans have produced films (especially documentaries), mounted photographic and art exhibitions, revived old and staged new dramatic productions and sponsored (privately-funded as opposed to official) acts of memorialisation.

This resurgence of interest in the Border War in the past five years or so is particularly remarkable given that the subject was virtually taboo during the preceding 15 years. While the new ruling party has constructed a triumphalist history of the liberation struggle to justify its legitimacy and the ANC's political ascendancy, the stories of UmKhonto weSizwe (MK) military veterans have not received that much attention. Like their SADF counterparts they regard themselves as marginalised and stigmatised.

But even without access to state resources SADF veterans have begun to affirm their contribution to the creation of the 'new' South Africa. This was patently evident in the furore that followed the decision of the trustees of Freedom Park to omit the names of deceased SADF veterans from its memorial walls. And it is less obvious yet equally remarkable in the exponential growth of publications about the Border War. This has allowed veterans to discover their own voices; to articulate counter-memories and narratives.

Catharsis seems to be a necessary rite of passage for the national service generation in the post-apartheid era. For some, at least, the emotional release of inner conflicts arising from military experience might offer a means of coming to terms with the past – that is, the intersection of personal stories and collective histories. The writer

Mark Behr exemplifies this process. His novel, *Die Reuk van Appels* (1993) – translated as *The Smell of Apples* (1995), tells of a young white Afrikaans-speaking boy being groomed to follow in his father's footsteps as a soldier in the militarised society that was apartheid South Africa. It frames the Border War within 'a brutal patriarchy that victimizes mothers and sons'.

Behr's revelation that he spied for the security forces while a student at the University of Stellenbosch underlined the cathartic purpose of his writing. His confessional narrative functions as an admission of guilt and an act of exculpation on his part. And his more recent novel, *Kings of the Water* (2009), makes an explicit link between militarisation, masculinity and his protagonist's forsaking of a heterosexual relationship in favour of a homosexual one. Behr remorselessly lays bare some of the paradoxes of Afrikaner society.

Memoirs written in English by former conscripts have tended to avoid introspection. Most of them have been written from (self-imposed) exile. They include Rick Andrew's *Buried in the Sky* (2001), Clive Holt's *At Thy Call We Did Not Falter* (2005), Steven Webb's *Ops Medic: A National Serviceman's Border War* (2008), Tim Ramsden's *Border-Line Insanity: A National Serviceman's Story* (2009) and Granger Korff's *19 With a Bullet: A South African Paratrooper in Angola* (2009). It would appear that the passage of time for reflection has given soldier-authors the space to make sense of their experiences and shape them into narratives. A number have managed to achieve a measure of healing while some are still dealing with traumatic memories.

These confessional texts by (sometimes) reluctant soldiers seldom admit complicity in upholding the apartheid system and in the event they do, the reason is not ideological convictions or patriotism but rather that they believed that they were duty bound to do so. Their life stories are frequently characterised by a telltale political naivety that suggests the SADF was waging a fully justified defensive campaign rather than an overtly aggressive colonial war. This trend has recently been bucked by medical doctor and psychiatrist Anthony Feinstein's *Battle Scarred: Hidden Costs of the Border War* (2011) which does not spare the security forces from criticism. Feinstein's text also stands out because of its literary qualities and astute observations about the legacy of the war.

The most popular of the 'confessional' texts has proved to be Jacqui Thompson's collection of conscripts' reminiscences, published under the title *An Unpopular War* (2006). These stories are recounted with a blend of honesty and self-delusion, candour and scepticism, and self-deprecating humour. Some are suffused with nostalgia for the 'good old days', while, contrarily, evincing a modicum of guilt about the part that the narrators played as perpetrators of violence and terror. The overwhelming impression is that these ex-soldiers see themselves as having simply performed their duties. But the book bears an inappropriate title, as the Border War was never unpopular among the majority of conscripts or with the white populace at large – although citizen force members increasingly sought to evade call-ups after the End Conscription Campaign gained some traction. Yet even during successive states of emergency in the 1980s, military service was still regarded by the majority as a necessary price to pay for white rule. Many of those who once supported the war do not now think it was worth fighting and this is evident in some of the stories told to the author. Hindsight is not so much an exact science as it is conscience-appeasing art.

Thompson's book has become a template for a series of similarly-styled collections of conscripts' stories. These include *Troepie: From Call-Up to Camps* (2009) and *From Soldier to Civvy: Reflections on National Service* (2010) by Cameron Blake. These stories are enriched by the addition of the insights of the women – the mothers, wives, and girlfriends – who were affected by the absence and, sometimes, the loss of their male soldiers. It is the unflinching honesty of some of these recollections that leaves the reader in little doubt that national service and participation in the Border War had a profound influence on white South Africans. Then and now.

So, where does *Somewhere on the Border* fit into the canon of Border War literature that I have constructed? Can we assess its significance simply by way of a reading of the text? Or do we need to take stock of its impact as theatre?

Performance offers audiences a more accessible enactment of the past than books, and has the potential not only to reinforce cultural ideologies but also to challenge them. The capacity of actors to shape historical understanding is circumscribed by the knowledge and interpretation that audiences bring to every performance. Scott Magelssen suggests that performers create space for the past in the moment of the present, simultaneously giving voice to 'those who have been silenced by other histories'.[2]

Somewhere on the Border expressed views contrary to apartheid orthodoxies. During the 1980s Akerman's play was regarded as an anti-war text written against the grain of the miltarisation of South African society. The ruling party was intent on creating a garrison state to combat the 'total onslaught' by the country's perceived enemies. Being under siege induced a laager mentality among white South Africans. In this atmosphere dissident voices were stifled or silenced altogether. As Akerman has shown in his preface, his script was treated with suspicion by the authorities and subjected to censorship before it could be staged in South Africa. When it was finally performed, *Somewhere on the Border* did much to raise awareness about the indefensibility of the apartheid system and the harmfulness of a militarised society. It confronted its audiences with some uncomfortable questions about the kind of society that was being created in South Africa.

Akerman was not the only artist critical of the SADF as an institution during the 1980s. A few SADF veterans with literary pretensions told their stories in thinly disguised fictionalised autobiographical works, especially in short stories, through the medium of Afrikaans. The genre of *grensliteratuur* not only related episodes about soldiers' experiences on remote borders it also highlighted the tensions that racked the country during the states of emergency.

The playwright Deon Opperman commented on the absurdities of the war in his dramatic work *Môre is 'n Lang Dag* (1986). With convincing characterisation and authentic dialogue he constructed a situation in which the conflict between his protagonists mirrors the contradictions of the wider South African society. Opperman has recently returned to the subject of national service by way of the nauseating nostalgia of his recent musical tribute *Tree Aan!*, which is a celebration of the national service generation's contribution to the South Africa of the present. Akerman has been content to revive *Somewhere on the Border*, which serves as a timely reminder that conscription left an indelible mark on the country's past.

Is *Somewhere on the Border* able to speak to audiences in our post-apartheid democratic order? What relevance, if any, might it have to the new generation of 'born frees'? In short, does *Somewhere on the Border* have resonance beyond its own time and place?

I believe that it does. This was confirmed when I attended a performance of the play at the National Arts Festival in Grahamstown in July this year. Peter Frost's review captured the divergent responses of the mixed – age, gender and race – audience with the observation that:

> Akerman's script is agonising to listen to after all these years and the nauseating humour is brilliant, but appalling. Indeed, knowing now what it was hiding, what it would mean, gives the play a dreadful third dimension; as the kids in the audience roared at the disgusting jokes, the older members stayed terribly, terribly still.[3]

As a former national serviceman I winced at the recall of the ribald humour, the denigration of women, the homophobic taunts, as well as the racism of the barracks banter. I cringed when reminded of the machismo and the false bravado of soldiers in an operational situation. I felt a deep sense of relief that my own sons had not been subjected to military service. Yet I realised how the play might facilitate inter-generational dialogue, especially between fathers and sons. While chatting with some of the cast after the show I was struck by how profoundly they were affected by their participation in the play. Although they had no military experience to speak of, they were able to identify with Akerman's characters. But above all I was overwhelmed by the conflicting emotions that the performance prompted in me and convinced that *Somewhere on the Border* still has something profound to say about the impact of the war on South African society.

I believe that the message of *Somewhere on the Border* will be filtered through the lens of a shifting, impressionistic historical consciousness about the war. During the 1980s few whites harboured misgivings about the justness of the war or the legitimacy of the apartheid state. Now there is considerable moral ambiguity about the war. For it is only in retrospect that some white South Africans have begun to ascribe new meanings to the Border War. This owes as much to its varied representation in the post-apartheid era as it does to the revival of earlier seminal works like *Somewhere on the Border*.

Lieden, 15 November 2011.

NOTES

1 Gary Baines is Associate Professor of History at Rhodes University, Grahams-town. He is co-editor of *Beyond the Border War: New Perspectives on Southern Africa's Late Cold War Conflicts* (2008).

2 Scott Magelssen 2011. 'Introduction' to Scott Magelssen & Rhona Justice-Malloy (eds), *Enacting History*. Tuscaloosa: University of Alabama Press, p 9.

3 Peter Frost. 2011. 'Shifting borders, pushing boundaries'. Available at: cue.ru.ac.za/theatre/2011/shifting-borders-pushing-boundaries.html

Printed and bound by CPI Group (UK) Ltd, Croydon, CR0 4YY

13/04/2025

14656582-0002